A Priest, a Prostitute, and Some Other Early Texans

Also by Don Blevins

Peculiar, Uncertain, and Two Egg
From Angels to Hellcats: Legendary Texas Women, 1836–1880
Texas Towns: From Abner to Zipperlandville

A Priest, a Prostitute, and Some Other Early Texans

THE LIVES OF FOURTEEN LONE STAR STATE PIONEERS

Don Blevins

LONE STAR BOOKS

Guilford, Connecticut

Helena, Montana

LONE STAR BOOKS

An imprint and registered trademark of Rowman & Littlefield

Distributed by NATIONAL BOOK NETWORK

Copyright © 2008 by Rowman & Littlefield
First Lone Star Paperback Edition, 2016

Front cover images (clockwise from center): (1) Wedding photograph of Hezekiah G. Williams and Lizzie Johnson, courtesy of the Austin History Center, Austin Public Library (2) Adah Isaacs Menken as Don Leon in *Children of the Sun*, courtesy of The Harvard Theatre Collection, Houghton Library (3) Martha White McWhirter from the Collection of the Lena Armstrong Public Library, Belton, Texas (4) Mollie Bailey and her favorite horse and buggy courtesy of Western History Collections, University of Oklahoma (5) Milton Faver on horseback courtesy of the Archives of the Big Bend, Bryan Wildenthal Memorial Library, Sul Toss State University, Alpine, Texas.

British Library Cataloguing-in-Publication Information available

Library of Congress Cataloging-in-Publication Data
The paperback edition of this book was previously cataloged by the Library of Congress as follows:

A priest, a prostitute, and some other early Texans : the lives of fourteen Lone Star State pioneers / Don Blevins.
   p. cm.
   Guilford, Conn. : TwoDot, c2008
   Includes bibliographical references (p. 165-181) and index.
   Contents: Father Michael Muldoon : Muldoon's Catholics — Sarah Bowman : she gave solace to many — in many ways — Aylett C. Buckner : they called him "Strap" — Sophia Porter : Paul Revere in a dress — Mollie Bailey : she played the center ring — Bass outlaw : Ranger Little Wolf — Lizzie Johnson Williams : educator, trail boss, rancher, miser — Wild man of the Navidad : "the thing that comes" — Adah Isaacs Menken : was she really naked? — Three-legged Willie : justice and independence above all — Madam Candelaria : was she at the Alamo—or wasn't she? — James Briton Bailey : he's still looking for his jug — Martha White McWhirter : she who was sanctified — Milton Faver : the baron of West Texas.
   ISBN 978-0-7627-4589-0 (pbk.)
   ISBN 978-1-4617-4720-8 (ebook)
   1. Pioneers—Texas—Biography. 2. Frontier and pioneer life—Texas—Anecdotes. 3. Texas—Biography. 4. Texas—History—Anecdotes.
976.4/050922 B
(OCoLC)ocn176926595

                                                                                    2009293347

ISBN 978-1-4930-2614-2 (pbk.)
ISBN 978-1-4930-2615-9 (ebook)

To My Family—Always

Contents

Preface

In January 1821 the Spanish government agreed to let an Anglo, Moses Austin, begin colonization of a section of its northern territory, Texas. Moses died before he could set his plans in motion, but his son Stephen assumed the mantle of *empresario*. By the end of the year, Mexico had gained its independence from Spain through a revolution instituted a decade earlier. Authorities in Mexico City decided to recognize the contract with Austin and permit it to remain in force.

There was no loyalty from Mexico in accepting the agreement between its former master and Austin. Those in power did so primarily for four reasons: (1) They were impressed by the way the Anglos had settled their Indian problem east of the Sabine River. (2) They saw how efficiently and quickly the Americans organized and put in place operational and functional settlements. (3) It was virtually impossible to get Mexican citizens to leave their homes south of Rio Bravo (Rio Grande) and move to the wild Texas hinterland. (4) Authorities believed that a small American settlement in Mexican territory would function as a buffer against further encroachment.

The events of 1836, when Texas declared its independence, proved this agreement to be a serious mistake for Mexico. Eventually, with the movement of America westward, there would have been conflict between the two entities. But that would have been in the unforeseeable future. As it turned out, the clash was set in motion several years earlier.

The opening of Texas for settlement drew hordes of Anglos from the east, across the Sabine River; from the north, across the Red River; and from the south, by water, through Galveston. In a relatively short time, Anglos outnumbered Mexicans in population. Cultural dislikes developed between the newcomers and the landed gentry almost from the outset. Although such animosities festered and grew, they were not revolutionary in nature. Actions by the central government in Mexico City would be the catalyst for upheaval by the Anglo colonists.

Travelers to the new paradise were of a varying breed. The overwhelming majority came for materialistic reasons—to make a new start, or to accrue a fortune. Some were dodging problems back home and posted the GTT (Gone to Texas) sign on their cabin doors as they raced from the law, spouses, or debtors.

Regardless of their reasons for migrating to Tejas, these people became part of the tapestry that evolved into the state as we know it today. Many of the blocks in the tapestry are still coming to light, and many more will arise as time marches on.

The fourteen pioneers profiled in this book—some well known, some unfamiliar—are part of that tapestry. One of the characters, Adah Menken, was in Texas for only a brief period yet made her mark on the entire state. Others came late in life, stayed around, and let the Texas dirt cover their final resting places. Molly Bailey did not reach Texas until she was over forty years of age. She became another block in the Lone Star tapestry.

These people were among the good and the bad, the gray and the dim. Remember, there was little law back in their times. They had to make their own way the best they could, especially the womenfolk.

They made their mark. They stayed the course. I don't know that we could have done as well. And for better or worse, they are part of Texas—and American—history.

Read and enjoy. And who knows? Maybe some of your ancestors are within these pages.

—Don Blevins
San Marcos, Texas

Father Michael Muldoon

MULDOON'S CATHOLICS

On Highway 77, across Interstate 10, just north of the city of Schulenburg, sits a weathered granite monument dedicated to "The Forgotten Man of Texas History." The marker honors Father Miguel (Michael) Muldoon, an Irish native who traveled East Texas in the early days preceding the Texas Republic. He was the only itinerant Catholic priest to serve the needs of Anglo settlers who migrated to the region of modern-day southeast Texas. There were other Catholic padres in the larger, predominantly Mexican/Spanish settlements of Nacogdoches (one priest), San Antonio de Béxar (two priests), and La Bahía (one priest). But clerics in those towns never ventured far from their dioceses, certainly not into the Anglo hinterland.

Father Muldoon officially appeared in Texas in 1831. However, the stage had been set a decade earlier for the presence of Catholic priests in the mainly Protestant Anglo enclave. On January 17, 1821, Spanish authorities in Monterrey, Mexico, granted Moses Austin permission to settle three hundred families from the United States in Texas. Austin, who had traveled to Texas to obtain this authorization, unfortunately never saw his quest materialize. On his eight-hundred-mile sojourn back to his home in Missouri, he ran into difficulties that ranged from robbery to lack of food to illness. He died, but one of his sons, Stephen F. Austin, stepped in to carry the baton. By the end of 1821, Mexico had gained its independence from Spain but allowed the colonization grant to carry forth.

With the grant came stipulations. The immigrants would be required to become Mexican citizens and to render support to the Mexican government as such citizenship levied. Another stipulation was the acceptance of Catholicism as the religion of the colonists. The first stipulation the settlers could pretty well accept, because most of them just wanted an opportunity either to start over or to make their fortunes. The settlers were overwhelmingly Protestant—at least those that followed any religion—but agreed to accept Catholicism, even if they did so with their hands behind their backs and their fingers crossed. The Mexicans were Catholic by birth, but many had seldom been in a church. They accepted the faith as their guiding light without viewing the church itself as the panacea to all personal and governmental difficulties.

The settlers composing the "Old Three Hundred" were legally bound to accept the Catholic faith, or promise to. The Anglos arriving later and seeking land grants just had to admit to being Christians—however loose the interpretation or acceptance. Protestant churches and official religious meetings were not allowed in the province, although, naturally, clandestine sessions took place in private homes.

Priests from the established churches in Nacogdoches, San Antonio de Béxar, and La Bahía would not leave the comfort and security of their surroundings. And then there was the matter of cost. Who would pay the expenses of a priest traveling to outlying settlements? The colonists, as part of the empresario agreement, were immune from taxes and other financial levies from Mexico City. The only allegiance the settlers had was to family and land, and not always in that order. They had no deity other than the one they wanted to worship, and they had practically no governmental restraint. In essence, they acquired a piece of land, they were free to work it and succeed or fail with little outside interference, and they literally rose or fell by the sweat of their brows.

Regardless of their benign neglect of a heavenly power, such recognition had to be considered. Without a religious representative to perform wedding ceremonies, children born of cohabitants could not inherit the land grants of their parents. Some measure was necessary to reach the Anglo settlers spread out over thousands of square miles. Onto the scene rode Father Muldoon. His first name was Miguel, but he assumed the anglicized "Michael" when in Texas. Due to the drawback of finances, Muldoon depended on the largesse of the settlers, not only for monetary payment but also for quarters and other sustenance.

Muldoon was born around 1780 in County Cavan, Ireland, located near the present-day border of Northern Ireland. Protestant England ruled the Land of Shamrocks; consequently, Catholicism was not in favor. Muldoon received his religious education in Catholic Spain, at the Irish College of Seville. (Another rendition of the priest's background is that his father, born in Dublin, Ireland, had a confrontation with the British military and had to flee the Emerald Isle. He ended up in Spain and married a Spanish woman—presumably making Miguel Spanish by birth, Irish by inheritance and inclination.)

Father Muldoon was up in years, for the time, past fifty when he asked for and received an assignment to the Diocese of Monterrey, Mexico. There he served as chaplain to Don Juan O'Donojo, the last Spanish viceroy (Mexico was on the brink of rebelling against its European overlords). The priest's first view of New Spain was his arrival on the continent in 1821, probably aboard a ship that docked at the port of Veracruz.

In Mexico City on business some years later, Stephen F. Austin had the opportunity to meet Muldoon. They experienced a natural liking for each other, and Father Muldoon was of great help to the empresario. The latter faced political roadblocks during his visit to the capital city and ran short of funds. Muldoon advanced Austin money to pay for lodging and food and also served as his Spanish tutor.

That the two men hit it off and became lifelong friends is well known. But Austin had an ulterior motive for cultivating the goodwill of the priest. Father Muldoon had inside access to Mexican officials high in the government. The empresario planned to use this access in the future.

Austin repaid his debt to Muldoon by helping him secure land in the territory. On May 31, 1831, the padre received title to eleven leagues, some 48,600 acres, in the area of present-day Fayette, Galveston, Lavaca, and Wharton Counties. Required to meet the same provision as other colonists, Muldoon built a stone hut on his land near the site of the hamlet of Muldoon, on FM Road 2237 in southwestern Fayette County, north of the town of Flatonia.

Father Muldoon was the first Catholic priest to serve non-Hispanics in Texas. He worked for a short time in what is now San Patricio County, situated along Corpus Christi Bay; he performed some marriage ceremonies there before returning to Mexico. His first official appearance in the territory occurred in April 1831. He departed in August 1832, but in that brief period the padre left his mark on the history of Texas. He used as his home base the village of San Felipe, where Austin made his home and headquarters.

In addition to administering baptisms and other blessings and sacraments, Father Muldoon was obliged to convert the colonists to the Catholic faith. Maybe the priest realized the futility of this chore, because he claimed that such individuals converted without the benefit of any training in the role and purpose of the Roman Catholic Church.

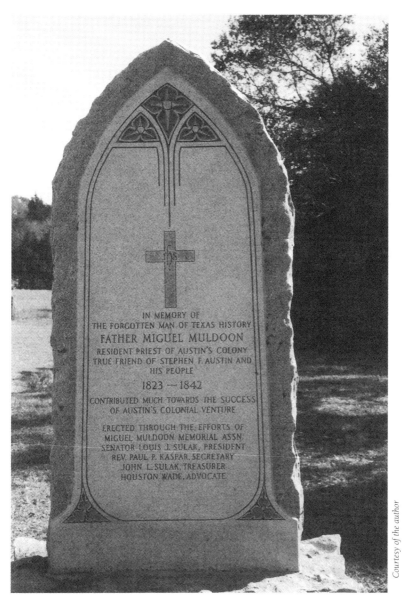

IN MEMORY OF
THE FORGOTTEN MAN OF TEXAS HISTORY
FATHER MIGUEL MULDOON
RESIDENT PRIEST OF AUSTIN'S COLONY
TRUE FRIEND OF STEPHEN F. AUSTIN AND
HIS PEOPLE
1823 — 1842
CONTRIBUTED MUCH TOWARDS THE SUCCESS
OF AUSTIN'S COLONIAL VENTURE

ERECTED THROUGH THE EFFORTS OF
MIGUEL MULDOON MEMORIAL ASSN.
SENATOR LOUIS J. SULAK, PRESIDENT
REV. PAUL P. KASPAR, SECRETARY
JOHN L. SULAK, TREASURER
HOUSTON WADE, ADVOCATE

Memorial for Father Muldoon, located south of La Grange on Highway 77

Those who experienced this conversion of convenience came to be called "Muldoon's Catholics."

The padre also conducted wedding ceremonies. Before his arrival in the settlement, neither all the saints in heaven nor all the mortals on earth could expect men and women to stay apart for months, or years, simply due to the lack of religious sanction of their union. Austin, who never married, realized this. The empresario convinced political chief José Antonio Saucedo to allow a sort of legalized "living in sin" situation for the settlers. Under this proviso a couple posted a bond (in essence a contract) that acknowledged their cohabitation, but they agreed to have the union sanctioned when a priest became available. These bonds, some as high as $10,000, were posted and the contract witnessed by the nearest alcalde (mayor). Austin wrote the first bond, which served as a matrix for future such documents, on April 29, 1824.

A unique stipulation in the contracts was that either or both parties could renege on the deal. The bonds were forfeited and both parties were then free to consider themselves single once again. From evidence of the day, "Many couples . . . not finding the marriage state to possess all the alluring charms which they had figured in their fond imagination, [took] advantage of this slip-knot plan—sought the bond, and by mutual consent committed it to flames—returned to the world as young as ever and free as the air."

The wedding ceremonies performed by Father Muldoon were serious affairs, in ritual if not in appearance. He often conducted the weddings of dozens of couples at a time. One such ceremony took place at the home of a Mrs. Williams, near the present-day community of West Point, a few miles west of La Grange. Some thirty people had gathered to be united by the rites administered by Muldoon. Such circumstances were not only expedient but also convenient, considering the distances people had to travel in those days. When all the ceremonies were completed, each couple that had exchanged vows received a certificate of marriage. The document was written in Latin on parchment and signed by Muldoon.

It was not unusual for a number of children to be present at the ceremonies. Some couples had been together long enough to have sired up to half a dozen offspring. Nor was it looked on as odd to see "brides . . . with bosoms open and little children sucking at the breast." Not all of those gathered for weddings considered them desirable or necessary. Many had been married by an alcalde and considered such an act legal and official. Nothing further was required to legalize an already legal matter, at least in their eyes.

Despite his friendship with Austin and his apparent affinity for Texians, Father Muldoon was a Catholic priest. In view of his position, he forbade all "bond" marriages. As a source of payment for services rendered, Muldoon charged $25.00, or something in kind, for a wedding and $2.00 for a baptism. This does not seem like much money today, but for colonizers who were land rich and cash poor, it certainly put a strain on the moneybag. The bonds, up to $10,000, would appear to be out of the reach of the vast majority of settlers, yet they managed to meet the financial levy.

Austin not only encouraged Father Muldoon's religious sojourns, but also accompanied the padre on several of his rounds. The more pious settlers looked on the mass weddings, despite the apparent support of the empresario, as disgraceful and sacrilegious. Some residents looked down their noses at Father Muldoon. They believed that the amount charged for weddings was exorbitant, that the padre was no more than a frocked buffoon. Even some later members of the Catholic Church had negative opinions of Muldoon.

To add to their distaste and distrust, the more conservative religious settlers viewed the padre as a fornicator and, in a derisive tone, accused him of associating with blacks in an unseemly manner. The priest's reputation did not improve in any way when he posted a notice in the colonist newspaper that he would "baptize and marry the black race of both sexes, without receiving from them or their masters any gratification."

Adding to this animosity was out-and-out distrust of the central government in Mexico City. The fear was that Mexico was attempting to force the colonists into the papal realm. The personality and general demeanor of the outgoing Irish priest dimmed this ill feeling, at least to some degree.

What bothered many of the settlers more was Muldoon's fulfillment of the Irish propensity to bend the elbow in jovial drink. The priest and John Barleycorn were on a first-name basis. Loud and boisterous, Father Muldoon enjoyed ending a hard day's work with several quaffs from the liquor cabinet.

The priest was said to be "addicted to alcohol" and had an "unlimited capacity for drink." And where better to carouse and cavort than on the wild Texas frontier of the early 1800s? Taverns were plentiful and served up all degrees of palatable ale and whiskey. For a man like the priest, this probably seemed like a version of heaven. But, like other men of the time and place, even the padre was not immune to run-ins and disagreements.

One story had him rambling with fellow drinkers and stopping at a saloon (or grocery store) owned by one Frank Adams. The owner invited Muldoon to have a drink with him. The priest turned up his nose at drinking with common riffraff and mistakenly verbalized his thoughts. Adams took such insults from no one. He proceeded to land a solid punch on Muldoon's nose. In reality, the tavern owner had struck a representative of the Mexican government. Father Muldoon chose to forgo any recrimination and to "apologize for his offensive language, and accept Adams's next drink offer as a way of 'taking his medicine.'"

Regardless of his foibles, the priest had a real and deep appreciation for the Texians and their goals. In 1832, in what became known as the Anahuac Disturbance, Muldoon attempted to quell the anger that arose when Mexico City levied taxes on merchandise at the port at Anahuac, situated on Trinity Bay in present-day Chambers County. Anglo colonists considered the establishment of the customhouse an illegal act and protested. Father Muldoon assisted Thomas Jefferson Chambers in protesting the action. Chambers was lawyer, state attorney, and chief justice. The priest helped write an objection (in Spanish) to the Mexican government disapproving of its established customhouse at Anahuac. Chambers County was named for the co-writer of the protest. The priest even offered his body in exchange for that of William Barrett Travis and some others who had been confined in jail in the Anahuac affair.

Following a show of force by the settlers, who were ready and willing to retaliate, the Mexican garrison in the fort at Velasco refused to let armed Anglos pass on their way to Anahuac. Muldoon tried to intervene to prevent bloodshed. He even entered the fort in an effort to persuade the garrison commander, Colonel Domingo de Ugartechea, to allow the militia to pass. The officer refused, and fierce fighting erupted on June 26. Three days later the Mexican troops ceded control of the fort, and the Anglos passed without further conflict.

Although Father Muldoon had many friends in high positions in Mexico, both military and political, he did not hesitate to speak his mind, even in the face of personal jeopardy. Upon his return to Mexico in August 1832, the priest espoused his support for the Texas cause and its call for less control from Mexico City. Winds of rebellion could be felt across the land. Less than four years later, Texas would be an independent republic.

In February 1834 Muldoon stepped in once again to help his old friend Austin. The empresario, a moderate who wanted peaceful relations with Mexico, had traveled to the capital to discuss issues that bothered the Anglo settlers. Austin's visit was peaceful in nature; his reception was not. Valentin Gómez Farías, acting president of Mexico, ordered Austin's arrest. The prisoner was held incommunicado for three months, his only visitor being Father Muldoon. The latter arranged bond for Austin, but Mexican officials rejected the offer.

Austin had earlier written an unwise letter to the *ayuntamiento* (municipal government) in San Antonio. In the missive, he suggested that San Antonio authorities assume leadership of all regional governmental units should hostilities with Mexico break out. It is not clear whether Austin anticipated an attack from Mexico. There was never any indication that the empresario intended revolt against the federal government. To the contrary, Austin took his position seriously and felt himself to be a citizen of Mexico. He did not believe that Texas should break away from the mother country, only that Texas deserved more independence.

Austin was confined in the worst of conditions and was even required to pay for his own food. William S. Parrott, an American merchant working with Austin, financed him with some $200 for food and drink. Muldoon also reportedly sent the prisoner cheese and drink and arranged for an innkeeper to provide food to Austin. The padre's humane endeavors did not end there. He journeyed to Manga de Clavo, where he spoke with President Antonio López de Santa Anna on Austin's behalf. Through Father Muldoon's effort, Austin finally was released from solitary confinement on May 9, 1834. Although Santa Anna recommended the prisoner be acquitted, freedom was not quick in coming—it was a year before Austin was released from prison, in the summer of 1835. He returned to Texas a changed man in attitude and determination.

Austin's once-moderate leaning now tilted in the opposite direction. The unwarranted detention by Mexican authorities, and their rigidity in refusing to discuss the colonists' grievances, left the future Father of Texas in a militant mood. Consequently, the winds of war began to blow even harder.

Two years after helping secure Austin's release from prison, Father Muldoon pulled off a feat so daring that it would appear to come from the imagination of a fiction writer—but it is fact. The padre and William H. Wharton, for whom Wharton County is named, were friends. Muldoon had spent many hours at the Wharton home, Eagle Island plantation, reveling in conversation, the full library of the Whartons, and, of course, liquid refreshments. Soon after Texas won its independence in April 1836, Wharton was appointed minister to the United States.

Wharton's assignment was to persuade the United States to annex Texas into the Union. There were two problems working against the Republic in its quest. First, Washington did not want a war with Mexico, which might occur should the United States take annexation action. Second, and probably more damaging, was the issue of slavery. Texas was a slave territory. No Northern legislator would vote to allow Texas to fly the Stars and Stripes as long as it remained a slave republic.

In April 1837 Wharton boarded the *Julius Caesar* in New Orleans en route to Texas after his failed mission in Washington. Two Mexican gunboats patrolled the Gulf of Mexico near the mouth of the Brazos River. The armed vessels stopped the ship on April 7, removed Wharton, and then took him to Mexico, where he was imprisoned in Matamoras. The Mexican justification for arresting Wharton was that he did not possess travel documents and was apprehended on open water in Mexican territory.

Once again, Father Muldoon was the only outsider allowed to visit the prisoner. The priest quickly realized that he would not be able to successfully negotiate Wharton's release, as he had for Austin. The Mexican attitude toward Anglos was angrier and more adamant. Taking a desperate step, and putting his own life in danger, Muldoon sneaked a priest's robe into Wharton's cell. The priest directed his friend, "Mr. Wharton. . . If you are accosted, simply extend your right hand with the first two fingers elevated and say 'Pax Vobiscum [peace be with you]'. Remember that you are a Catholic priest until you reach Texas." So garbed and so advised, Wharton simply walked out of the prison and headed north. A short time later, he crossed into the Lone Star Republic.

For official purposes, Father Muldoon's visits to Texas had ended in 1832. However, he did make scattered unofficial returns to the region. In early 1836 he ransomed a Mrs. Juergens from Indian captivity, after a raid on the dying settlement of Port Oak Point in Fayette County. And in April 1839 the priest performed a wedding in Houston. At the time he held the title of Catholic Vicar General of the Republic of Texas. Muldoon thought more of his position, however, and carried the self-proclaimed title of D. D. Vicar General of the Catholic Communities of the Free and Independent Republic of Texas.

In April of that same year, Muldoon volunteered to accompany Colonel Bernard E. Bee Sr. on the diplomatic sojourn to Mexico. Three years after the Battle of San Jacinto, it appeared that the Federalists, now in power in Mexico, were amenable to recognizing the independence of Texas. It was Bee's assignment to secure this recognition, and he had the authority to offer the Mexican government $5 million for it. The Rio Grande would serve as the international boundary. Father Muldoon went with Bee to serve as interpreter and to grease the diplomatic skids. They departed New Orleans aboard the schooner *Woodbury* on May 2; six days later they sailed into Veracruz.

Due to the vagaries of the Mexican government at the time, Santa Anna was missing from the top rung of power in Mexico; General

Anastasio Bustamante occupied the tenuous, and temporary, seat of president. Bee stayed in the port city for ten days waiting to hear from authorities in Mexico City. But Bustamante would not meet with Bee and even threatened to imprison the Texian, who subsequently sailed for home. For his part, the good padre did not possess enough grease or influence with the Mexican president. The deal fell through.

For his involvement in the official activities of Texas, as they concerned Mexico, and his open support for the Texas cause, Mexican authorities placed Father Muldoon behind bars in March or April of 1839. Realizing the quagmire that could result from accusing a Catholic priest of sedition, officials charged Muldoon with the less severe and almost laughable act of leaving Mexico without appropriate travel papers.

Muldoon's treks across the Rio Grande did not cease because of all the brouhaha. In 1842 he was in Austin, where Republic representatives recognized the padre for his service to Texas and Texians. From all indications, this was Father Muldoon's last trip to the Republic.

Muldoon's final years and cause of death are a mystery. This seems to be the case for many people who traversed Texas in the early and mid-1800s. According to some reports, Santa Anna imprisoned the padre after Muldoon's return from Texas in 1842. The Napoleon of the West was a vengeful dictator and could have easily turned from friend to dangerous foe, even to a Catholic priest. The rumored cause of Santa Anna's ire was the fact that Muldoon had aided Wharton's escape from prison. But a five-year span is a long time before taking action against someone the Mexican leader surely regarded as a traitor. Muldoon had crossed the Rio Grande a number of times since 1835 and could have been arrested at will.

Others believe that the priest met foul play during one of his travels, or that while sailing back to Spain he fell overboard and drowned. Along the latter line, heirs of Father Muldoon claimed that the priest was shipwrecked while sailing between New Orleans and Veracruz. They asserted that the land grants ceded to him had not been reallocated at the time of his death. In the mid- or late 1830s, Father Muldoon asked Austin to sell his Texas land; the property was disposed of for $5,000. The Padre's relatives filed suit as early as 1877 to have the land returned to the family. The courts rejected the claims. The suit was dismissed.

Until a viable claim is made as to the accurate death of Father Muldoon, let us put him on the veranda of a villa in sunny Spain, a glass of vino in one hand, a book in the other. His thoughts, though, are not on the book. They are hundreds of miles away, westward, as he reflects on his days in that wild, strange land called Texas.

Sarah Bowman

SHE GAVE SOLACE TO MANY—IN MANY WAYS

Sarah Bowman, like so many women—and men—who traversed Texas in the nineteenth century, was an enigma. She was married many times, probably most without legal or religious sanction. She had a number of surnames, including but not limited to Borginnis, Bourjette, Bourget, Bourdette, Bowman, Bowman-Phillips, Davis, and Foyle. She might have been born in Tennessee but more than likely first saw life in Clay County, Missouri, on June 5, 1812. Like many women of the time, Sarah could neither read nor write. Yet she owned and operated hotels, eateries, brothels, and other enterprises, most of them successful. She also became proficient in the Spanish language.

Born under the name of Sarah Knight, the first thirty-three years of her life are blank. She supposedly accompanied General Zachary Taylor and his troops to Florida during the Seminole War of 1837. She did not emerge onto the scene of public record, however, until 1845. Sarah was married to a soldier, John Langwell, whom she wed sometime in the 1840s. She traveled with him when he was part of Taylor's army that gathered at Corpus Christi, Texas, preparatory to what would become the Mexican-American War. When Texas joined the American Union on December 29, 1845, the action was tantamount to a declaration of war, from Mexico's point of view. Additionally, the boundary between Texas, now the United States, and Mexico was unclear: Was it the Rio Grande, as claimed by Texas and the United States, or the Nueces River, several miles north of the Rio Grande, as claimed by Mexico?

Sarah was an imposing figure, standing six feet, two inches in height and weighing in at around two hundred pounds. She was described as being "dark eyed with enormous breasts and an hourglass figure," assets that did not escape the notice of the men around her. For example, Trooper George Washington Traherne, a soldier in the Mexican-American War, indelicately described Sarah like so: "You can imagine how tall she was . . . she could stand flat footed and drop those little sugar plums [nipples] right into my mouth."

Legendary Texas Ranger John Ford spoke of Sarah more eloquently, declaring, "She could whip any man, fair fight or foul, could shoot a pistol better than anyone in the region, and at black jack could out play (or out cheat) the slickest professional gambler." Sarah earned the sobriquet "the Great Western," probably while she was in South Texas. The nickname referred to a British-owned vessel, one of the largest steamships of the 1830s, and only the second ship to sail the Atlantic Ocean sans sails, relying on steam alone.

Sarah proved her mettle on several occasions around military men and drove home the point that she was not one to be messed with. One soldier who whistled at her and made some off-color remark quickly paid for his indiscretion. The Great Western "whisked with the litheness of a panther. . . . Before the startled heckler knew what was happening, she had hoisted him like a sack of feathers and pinned him high against the side of a wooden building." According to author Mercedes Graf, Sarah held him there, his feet dangling above the ground.

Finally, the soldier eked out a quiet apology. Graf notes, "The woman's face was a granite mask. Suddenly she dropped her hand and the unhappy trooper plummeted back to earth. The woman turned abruptly and stalked away—she had not uttered a single word during the entire incident."

Neither the soldier brought to his knees, nor any witnesses, would fail to exert great caution around her in the future.

Military rules in Sarah's time were lax where soldiers' wives were concerned. It was permissible for the spouses of enlisted personnel to accompany the army and serve as laundresses and cooks. A rumor was bandied about that Sarah was in love with General Taylor and that by accompanying her husband, she could be near the man she truly cared for. If the rumor was fact, then it was apparently one-sided adoration; there is no record that Old Rough and Ready exhibited any amorous feeling in return.

Sarah's lack of fear came to the forefront many times. When peace negotiations between Mexico and the United States fell apart, General Taylor moved his troops toward the Rio Grande. Most of the women that had been traveling with the army moved to Port Isabel, some forty miles northeast of present-day Brownsville, for their safety. Not so the Great Western. With the help of some of the young officers, Sarah secured a mule and a cart, loaded it with cooking utensils and supplies, and in the fashion of the best teamsters of the day followed the Seventh Infantry on its march to the Rio Grande.

The first meeting of American and Mexican troops in battle took place on March 21, 1846, at the Paso Real crossing of Arroyo Colorado. Sarah offered to swim the arroyo and "whip the enemy single handedly." She probably would have tried if the military commander had seen fit to accede to her wishes. However, General William Worth, whom the city of Fort Worth honors in name, declined

Courtesy of the author

Grave marker for Sarah Bowman in the National Cemetery, Presidio, CA.

to see the woman commit what assuredly would have been sui-
cide.

Sarah's husband's unit was transferred to Fort Texas, located at
the extreme southern tip of Texas, across the Rio Grande from Matamoros. (The military installation was later renamed Fort Brown in
honor of Major Jacob Brown, who was killed on May 9, 1846, by
Mexican troops bombarding the fort from Matamoros.) General Taylor
had to take most of his troops to Port Isabel to stop a possible invasion
by Mexican troops that would seriously interrupt American commu-
nications. Left behind to finish building and to protect Fort Texas was
the Seventh Infantry, commanded by Major Brown.

While at Fort Texas, Sarah refused to let enemy fire curtail what she considered her duty to the American soldiers. A safe haven was prepared in an underground storage bunker for the remaining women of the fort. Sarah declined to use the bunker and continued to cook and supervise the mess facilities for a week during the bombardment. At one point "a tray was shot from her hand and a stray shell fragment pierced her sunbonnet," according to the *Portable Handbook of Texas*. She continued her chores unfazed and undeterred.

In spite of the demands on her time and energy and the danger all around, Sarah managed to feed the women hidden in safety, as well as care for wounded soldiers. Yet domestic chores were not her only contribution to the cause. She also acquired a musket and was prepared to join in the defense of the fort. Her willingness proved unnecessary, however. For bravery in the face of danger, she received another nickname: the Heroine of Fort Brown.

General Taylor returned with the bulk of his army, and the Mexican forces were quickly routed. The American troops moved into and occupied Matamoros, now devoid of any sign of Mexican forces. A banquet was held in June 1846 to celebrate the great victory. Several toasts were rendered, honoring President Polk, General Taylor, and the many young officers who had fought so gallantly in the battle. Lieutenant Braxton Bragg, a future general in the Confederate Army during the Civil War (and the namesake of Fort Bragg, North Carolina), rose and proffered a toast different from any of the others. He raised his glass in "a toast to the 'Heroine of Fort Brown.' All jumped to their feet with thunderous cheers . . . to drink to the Great Western and shatter their glasses against the walls."

The might of the American army was virtually unstoppable. So was Sarah. When the military moved across the Rio Grande and entered Mexican territory, so did she. She is believed to have opened and briefly operated a hotel in Matamoros before moving west with the Seventh Infantry. As usual, she drove her wagon, now pulled by small Mexican ponies, carrying the necessities for operating her mess. She opened a second hotel in Monterrey and a third in Saltillo, some 175 miles west of Matamoros. What American would be so brazen as to open a hostelry deep inside enemy territory? Sarah was. To add salt to the wound, she had the gall to christen her enterprise the American House.

In her facilities of rest and relaxation, she provided the soldiers with food, drink, and women. Where the women came from is unexplained. American women were rare in hostile Mexico, and Mexican *rameras* (prostitutes) would not likely ply their trade for the hated gringos, even for good money. Sarah did employ Mexicans and blacks as servants and was not very nice to either, reportedly knocking "them about like little children."

While near Monterrey, Sarah became involved in the action of the Battle of Buena Vista, which took place on February 22 and 23, 1847. She not only loaded rifles and handguns, but also ventured onto the battlefield and carried wounded soldiers to safety. Her nursing skills earned her the title of Doctor Mary, and supposedly she was awarded a government pension for her actions on the warfront, although there is no record of such grant. When Sarah learned that Captain George Lincoln, a friend of hers, had been killed during the battle, she took it upon herself to seek out his body from among the dead. Successful in her endeavor, Sarah carried the body back to her hotel in Saltillo and ensured that Lincoln received a proper burial.

Sarah and Lincoln were friends of some years' standing, and she mourned his death. It was the captain who had administered the oath of enlistment to Sarah's first husband at Jefferson Barracks in Missouri. Sarah reportedly paid about $250 for Lincoln's horse, then had it shipped to his relatives in Boston.

The whereabouts of Sarah's husband at this time are unknown. He might have been killed in battle, or he could have deserted the Great Western. It could just as well be that Sarah deserted him.

American and Mexican representatives signed a peace treaty at the village of Guadalupe Hidalgo, near Mexico City, on February 2, 1848. Sarah had kept the American House in operation all this time and had picked up a new husband. Not surprisingly, his name is an uncertainty, with varying sources citing it as Bourjette, Bourget, or Bourdette. He was assigned to the United States Fifth Infantry. Five months after the end of the war, Sarah was ready to head home. However, she quickly ran into a snag.

Her second husband was no longer in the picture because of either death or desertion. When Sarah expressed interest in traveling north with the American military contingent, she was advised that only married women could move with the army. Not one to suffer rejection, Sarah mounted her horse and rode among the troopers, who were in formation. As she rode she bellowed, "Who wants a wife with $15,000 and the biggest leg in Mexico? Come, my beauties, don't speak all at once. Who is the lucky man?"

Most of the troopers probably had no desire to hook up with the Amazon. They certainly were not anxious to be within arm's reach should she get mad. Silence prevailed until a dragoon named Davis (or David E.; the historical record is unclear) spoke. He had one stipulation: that a man of the cloth sanction the wedding. Sarah laughed and responded, "Bring your blanket to my tent tonight and I will learn you to tie a knot that will satisfy you, I reckon." Did a religious representative perform a wedding? Who knows? Regardless of her marital status, Sarah marched off with the Americans as they headed north.

A short time later Sarah was in Franklin (present-day El Paso). She opened another hotel, this time on the Ponce de Leon Ranch, which was owned by Benjamin Franklin Coons, a teamster and merchant who suffered many financial ups and downs during his lifetime. The year was 1849. Some four thousand gold seekers patronized Sarah's inn on their way to California. Forever the entrepreneur, Sarah offered her transient guests comfort in the way of food and "entertainment." To many who knew her, she was the "whore with a heart of gold," and it is possible that she holds the dubious distinction of being the first American prostitute in El Paso.

People who were acquainted with Sarah knew how to handle themselves in her presence. Those unfamiliar with her personality and loyalties could suffer dire consequences. One day an American soldier ran into Sarah's Saltillo, Mexico, hotel. Panting and gasping, he sputtered that General Taylor had been resoundingly defeated in the battle of Buena Vista.

That was the last bit of information to come from the man's mouth for some time. Sarah floored him with a sledgehammer punch. Standing over the dazed victim, she said, "You damned son of a bitch! There ain't Mexicans enough in Mexico to whip old Taylor!" Looking down at him, she continued, "You just spread that report and I'll beat you to death." Sarah had been at the battle and knew the words the soldier spat out were untrue.

Sarah's length of stay in El Paso is unknown. She set out for Socorro, New Mexico, after leasing her hotel to the United States Army. By this time Davis was out of the picture and Sarah had moved on to her fourth husband, Albert J. Bowman. Several years younger than Sarah, Albert was from Germany and was a sergeant in the Second Dragoons.

Following his discharge on November 30, 1850, the couple relocated to what is now Yuma, Arizona, where Sarah opened a boarding house that provided the usual female diversion. A local priest, Father Figueroa, noted that Sarah was the first American woman proficient in the Spanish language to settle in the area. He evaluated her character from a benevolent bent, as people of the cloth are prone to do. The padre declared Sarah "a good hearted woman, good soul old lady . . . "

Nevertheless, rumors circulated that she was carrying on a sexual relationship with Colonel Samuel P. Heintzelman, the commander of Fort Yuma—and a married man. The commander and Sarah did not mesh too well at the outset. She cooked for some of the officers but did not ask the commander to attend the dinner festivities. Naturally, this infuriated Heintzelman, and he was not too kind to her in his journal entries. Yet in January and February of 1854, she and the commander started getting closer.

Although Sarah was a rough-and-tumble individual, she did have a compassionate streak. Unable to have children of her own, she adopted several from both sides of the border. On occasion she had to move to Mexico to protect her Latino children. (Apparently, relatives of some of the children Sarah adopted had serious misgivings about the youngsters being placed in the care of a prostitute.) She secured the aid of Heintzelman to move to Mexico as needed. While south of the border, she opened another hotel, and one of her recurring visitors was the Yuma post commander.

Their affair ended in July 1854. After some contentious bargaining with the colonel, Sarah bought some of his animal stock and household effects. Heintzelman was reassigned to another post the same month.

By some accounts, a dark and seamy side to Sarah surfaced while she was in Yuma. Word spread that Sarah was using young girls, some under the age of ten, in her prostitution enterprise. There were even hints that her adopted young children were involved in the pursuit of ill-gotten gains. Whispers abounded that Colonel Heintzelman was a recipient of bordello pleasures south of the border.

Sarah and Albert sold their homeplace and business enterprises in 1857 and moved to Patagonia, southeast of Tucson. She continued with the occupations she knew best: a hotel and brothel. This time, though, she also opened a saloon.

By the mid-1860s Sarah and Albert were no longer together. Their separation did not curtail her association with the army, through which she received a military ration and for which she served as company laundress. Sarah traveled between Fort Buchanan and Yuma (at that point called Arizona City) and was back in the latter by 1861.

Sarah continued with the inn and restaurant business but apparently had sideline interests as well. Some referred to her as "the greatest whore in the West." Lieutenant Sylvester Mowry, stationed at Fort Yuma in 1856, declared that "among her other good qualities she was an admirable pimp." This presumably was a favorable attribute of the day.

Sarah Bowman, or whoever she really was, met her end around the age of fifty, in the mid-1860s (various sources list her death date as December 1863 or December 1866). What bullets and bombs could not do, one of nature's creatures did: The bite of a tarantula brought on her demise. Authorities laid her to rest in the Fort Yuma base cemetery, the only woman to be so honored. Not only was she interred in military ground, she also received full military honors. To receive that recognition she must have kept the soldiers' clothes especially clean or cooked some very enticing meals.

More than likely, her past efforts on behalf of the soldiers in Corpus Christi, at Fort Brown, and in Mexico earned Sarah such recognition. The Quartermaster Department of the United States Army extended the honor in August 1890, when it exhumed the 159 bodies interred at Fort Yuma. All were moved to the Presidio in San Francisco, California. Sarah was among them.

Arthur Woodward, one of Sarah's biographers, said after her burial that she was "a woman of kind heart and great bravery—one hell of a good woman." Remembered by some, unknown by many, forgotten by most, Sarah Bowman had her run at events of the day. She marked her trail; she followed it. Sarah asked no quarter; no quarter was given. Few people ever travel that road.

Aylett C. Buckner

THEY CALLED HIM "STRAP"

Aylett Buckner was born in Louisa County, in west-central Virginia, around 1794, the son of Aylett and Elizabeth Buckner. He died in Texas in 1832. Few people ever put so much adventure and living into a short thirty-eight years as did Aylett.

Aylett was an adventurer—a soldier of fortune, as it were. He served as a filibuster, militia commander, and Indian fighter and even settled down for a period as a farmer, which he had to find dull and uninviting. Although his physical dimensions are unknown, he must have been large and powerful in appearance. At least one report lists him as six feet, six inches tall and weighing about 250 pounds. Friends and neighbors in Virginia nicknamed him "Strap" because of his size and prowess. This is a Southern term, bestowed on one whose physique would fit in with weight lifters of today.

It is said that Strap "hunted the strongest game with no other weapon than his bare fist; and the wildcat, wolf, and bear soon became scarce in the Colorado lowlands" of Texas. He was apparently a kind man and unaware of what his muscular frame could do, regardless of how innocently intended. Writer Annette Ruckert notes that Strap "playfully slapped men on the back with such force as to cause bruises and injury. . . . he knocked men down without the least intention of doing them harm."

Strap came to Texas as a member of the Gutíerrez-Magee expedition (organized by José Bernardo Gutíerrez de Lara and Augustus W. Magee), which aimed to separate Texas from Spain and took place during the Mexican unrest against Spanish domination. The filibusters crossed the Sabine River on August 8, 1812. Although he was only about eighteen years old at the time, Strap's size belied any youthful appearance.

At first, success was sweet to the invaders, but soon turmoil within the ranks weakened their efforts. When the Spanish rallied their forces, it spelled doom for the insurgents. By late August 1813 Spanish royalist forces had overwhelmed the filibusters. Many were able to escape back to Louisiana, but more than five hundred faced the firing squad. Strap was one of the lucky ones and made it safely across the Sabine. Financially broke from his filibuster activity, Strap captained a riverboat, sailing between New Orleans and Natchez, Mississippi. (It was on one of the trips, while docked at Natchez, that he reportedly first met Stephen F. Austin; the colonizer booked passage on Strap's boat in late 1821.)

Four years later, with Strap's quest for adventure still controlling his emotions, he was back in Texas with the Francisco Xavier Mina excursion. Encouraged by American military leader General Winfield Scott and Mexican liberal Father José Servando Teresa de Mier Noriega y Guerra, Mina took on the task of abetting the independence of Mexico from Spain. With much backing from various American interests and an army of some two hundred men, Mina landed in Mexico on April 15, 1817. His army had small victories at the outset, as had earlier expeditions. But Mina was captured by Spanish forces on October 27, taken to Mexico City, and executed at Fort San Gregorio. Again, Strap escaped.

"Strap" Buckner by Ann Brightwell, based on research of written records

In 1819 Strap took part in his third and final filibuster venture. He accompanied Dr. James Long on an expedition to free Texas from Spanish rule. Long resided in Natchez, Mississippi, as did Strap. In June 1819 a provisional government, with Long at its head, met in Nacogdoches and declared the independence of Texas. Four months later, the "freedom" was over and Long and his surviving followers were back on the eastern side of the Sabine, chased there by Spanish troops. Not to be deterred, Long took up the filibustering cause again in April 1820. Victory was sporadic at best, and Long and a number of his men were captured. He was taken to Mexico City, where around March of 1822 he was shot and killed, either by accident or in a clandestine plot. Once more, Strap made it safely back to the United States.

In 1821 Strap joined up with Peter Powell and Oliver Buckner (relationship, if any, unknown) and settled on Buckner's Creek, south of present-day La Grange, Fayette County. Strap always boasted that he erected the first cabin on the Colorado River, into which Buckner's Creek flows. No one disputed his claim or challenged his assertion that "he had lost more property to Indian depredations than anyone else on the river." In 1824 Strap became one of Stephen F. Austin's Old Three Hundred, the original settlers in Austin's colony. On July 24 of that year, he was granted title to one *sitio* (a little over four thousand acres) of land, and a month later he came into possession of two *labores* (about 354 acres). His property was located in what became Matagorda County.

Strap and Austin were congenial, if not close. In mid-1824 the empresario sent Strap as part of a powwow party to treat with the Waco and Tawakoni Indians, near Waco. Any agreement reached was not put in writing, and the oral pact was soon broken. A year after Strap received his land grants, he and Austin had a falling out. The bone of contention was the amount of land Strap had been granted and its location. He penned a letter to Austin outlining his grievances for not receiving additional land and even threatened to bypass Austin in his quest and appeal directly to Mexican authorities in San Antonio.

Strap put on paper words that a number of colonists felt in their resentment of Austin. Several, like Strap, considered themselves legal squatters and occupied land before Austin received colonial approval for settlement from Mexico City. They did not take it lightly that the empresario was charging for land he had received free. Mexico authorized Austin to charge fees and other reimbursements in his colony, but regardless of how cheap acreage was compared to land in the United States, to cash-poor settlers, any amount was a strain.

Disagreement between the two became so rancorous that Austin threatened to have Strap arrested. Austin even alerted Andrew Rabb, another member of the Old Three Hundred, that he might be called upon to clamp the insolent settler in irons. In fact, Austin directed Rabb to take custody of Strap and bring him to San Felipe, the empresario's headquarters.

After receiving Austin's command, Rabb suddenly become ill. Whether this "illness" was a real ailment or simply came about because Rabb sympathized with Strap, as did many other colonists, is unknown. Maybe Rabb had no desire to tangle with Strap, who had defied Austin to try to arrest him. Regardless, after consulting with other colonists, Austin cooled off, and he and Buckner worked out a mutually acceptable agreement.

The relations between Strap and Austin improved to the point that in January 1826, the empresario appointed Strap as a judge, along with Moses Morrison and William Kincheloe, to oversee the election of the *alcalde* (mayor) for Mina (present-day Bastrop). Later that same year, Strap traveled to Matamoros, Mexico. He wanted to put in a claim for his services during the Gutierrez and Mina filibusters, since he had fought in Mexico's interest. It is unknown whether his effort bore fruit, although the Mexican government did recognize his participation in the two expeditions.

Austin also made Strap a military commander; as such, he was charged with warding off attacks by regional Indians. Strap was in the group that, in the winter of 1826, retaliated against a band of Karankawa Indians believed guilty of killing the Elisha Flowers and Charles Cavanaugh families. Likewise, he was at the forefront of an attack against the same Indian tribe at Live Oak Bayou, in eastern Matagorda County, in 1831. The Karankawa had killed Charles Cavanaugh's wife and three of his four daughters. When Strap's unit caught up with the Indians, the Texians attacked, firing at anything that moved, including women and children. Some forty or fifty Karankawa were killed. A small tribe to begin with, the Karankawa virtually disappeared after this battle.

Earlier, sometime in 1822, Strap had instigated a little chicanery that he hoped would bring about the eradication of both the Karankawas and the Tonkawas. He owned a trading post and discreetly sold arms and ammunitions to both tribes, keeping the transactions with one secret from the other. When the two tribes met face to face on an open prairie, it was Strap's hope that they would kill off each other. His hopes failed to materialize, however. The Indians were not proficient with the white man's weapons, so all that arose that day was a thick pall of smoke over the area; only a handful of Indians from both sides suffered injury.

In December 1826 Strap's allegiance to Austin was tested when Benjamin and Haden Edwards, who had settled on land grants around Nacogdoches, in East Texas, fomented what came to be called the Fredonian Rebellion. The brothers tried to run their empresorial grant like a small kingdom, even threatening early settlers with the loss of land they had lived on for some time. They also crossed swords with the

Mexican government and appealed to other Anglo colonists to join their side of the battle. Believing that Strap was no friend of Austin, Benjamin tried to enlist Strap to help him in the filibuster. Strap not only refused to join in the assault, but also signed a resolution protesting the action of the Edwards brothers. This gesture cemented the friendship between Strap and Austin, and it lasted the rest of their lives.

Most of the colonists considered themselves loyal Mexican citizens (at least for land grant and settlement reasons) and refused to aid what they considered an insurrection. Many Anglos marched with Mexican forces to Nacogdoches. When this combined army showed up on January 31, 1827, the Fredonian Rebellion quickly became history, and the perpetrators scrambled over each other crossing the Sabine, heading east.

Strap might have finally had the chance to settle down thereafter, but the record shows that he never married. An Indian tribe, the story goes, arranged a marriage between the white man and Tulipita, an Indian princess, but Strap begged off. Nevertheless, the Indians were so impressed by his powerful physique that they nicknamed him "Red Son of Blue Thunder," apparently influenced not only by his physical appearance, but by his shock of red hair as well.

A man of such physical proportions as Buckner, and without any family to verify or deny his feats, was certain to leave a legacy of part fable and part truth. In Texas, a land where myth and fact comfortably walk hand in hand, the feats of Strap Buckner were accepted, if with a wink. Among the fables left behind was his conquering of Triste Noche, a ferocious bull that threw scares into the settlers. After this successful confrontation, lore has it that Strap challenged old Satan himself to a duel.

Despite his physical prowess and the legends that arose around him, Strap was not invincible. On June 25 or 26, 1832 (records are unclear), he came face to face with the grim reaper, and the latter won. Strap died in the Battle of Velasco, located in what is today part of Brazosport, in southern Brazoria County.

Velasco is recognized as the first military engagement between Texians and Mexican forces. On June 26, 1832, John Austin and Henry Smith led a contingent of Texian militia to Brazoria to secure two cannons. The weapons were to be used against Mexican troops in Anahuac. Mexico had established a port of entry at Velasco, and it was garrisoned by Mexican troops under the command of Colonel Domingo de Ugartechea. The commander ordered the ship carrying the Anglos and the cannons to stop. The Texians refused. No one knows how many people were on each side of the conflict; the Texians supposedly numbered between 100 and 150, the Mexican garrison anywhere from 91 to 200.

When the Texians refused to halt, fighting erupted. William Jarvis Russell, commander of the schooner *Brazoria,* is said to have fired the first shot of the Texas Revolution when he sent salvos into the Mexican defenses. The Texians came out ahead because the Mexican forces ran out of ammunition and had to surrender. Mexican and Texian representatives signed a document on June 29 that called for cessation of firing and allowed the Anglo ship to continue up the Brazos, with its cargo intact. Ugartechea and his men were treated honorably and allowed to return to Mexico, with the Anglos even providing a ship for them.

As with the total number of combatants involved in the melee, the number of casualties on both sides is unknown. It is believed that the Mexicans suffered five dead and sixteen wounded. Guesstimates for the Anglo side are seven killed and fourteen wounded; three of the latter died of their wounds sometime later. Strap Buckner was killed during the first day of battle.

Strap's legendary strength gained more fame at Velasco. The Texians shaped shields out of three-inch cypress wood. Since cypress is a hard and heavy wood, it took four men to tote the shields—but Strap carried one by himself. The shields proved to be poor defensive implements against Mexican bullets. One bullet pierced the shield Strap was brandishing and sent splinters into his face and head; he died instantly.

Despite Strap's participation in the early history of Texas, and especially Fayette and Matagorda Counties, there are no memorials to his deeds or even to his existence. In fact, no one seems to know where Strap was finally laid to rest.

Strap left no family to record the events of his life. What did come forth emerged mostly from tales told around campfires and from tobacco-chewing settlers sitting beside potbellied stoves in small country stores. Strap's size, ferocity, fearlessness, and quick temper (which was just as quick to cool) stoked the fires of midnight tales long after he had breathed his last.

What would Aylett Buckner have accomplished had he survived Velasco? Who knows? But you can rest assured that he would have been in the thick of things at Goliad, or the Alamo, or San Jacinto. Strap could not be held back; he gave his all, and that inevitably included his life.

Sophia Porter

PAUL REVERE IN A DRESS

On the northern edge of Texas is 89,000-acre Lake Texoma, its name defining the two states that share this water sports paradise. And on a finger of land jutting into the blue water is a spot called Preston Point. In the 1800s, long before the site became a watery grave, the matron of Glen Eden Plantation gained quite a reputation— both good and unsavory.

Sophia Suttenfield, one of seven children born to William and Laura Suttenfield, first saw daylight on December 3, 1815, in Fort Wayne, Indiana. Born of humble parentage, Sophia always had an eye for the better things. Her father was a bartender in a local saloon and had once served as a regular soldier in the American army. However, when Sophia spoke of him, she often promoted him to colonel. Sophia satisfied most of her yearnings thanks to good looks, intelligence, and a canny ability to know how and when to use her natural talents.

When she was eighteen years old, Sophia eloped with Jesse Augustine Aughinbaugh. The wedding date, according to author Gelnna Parker Middlebrooks, was July 14, 1833. Jesse arrived the previous year to assume the position as headmaster of Allen County seminary, which Sophia attended. Why Jesse lingered only a short time in

Fort Wayne is unknown. Perhaps his reasons were financial: Apparently, the teaching profession, then as now, was not very lucrative. Or perhaps he was forced to resign from the seminary. The only teacher in town, he was also Catholic—and this combination did not sit right with many of the town's Protestant community pillars. Regardless, Jesse left the field of education and became head of a self-named drug firm: J. A. Aughinbaugh and Company.

Just as she improved her father's biography, Sophia asserted that Jesse had been an officer of some prestige in the German army. There was no substantiation for this claim. The consensus is that he was a sutler, or salesman, that followed military troops, selling them supplies along with whatever he could pass off as whiskey.

Through word of mouth, Jesse and Sophia soon heard of the vast, almost limitless quantities of Mexican land in a place called Tejas. Adventurous or simply looking for fortunes, they shook the dust of Indiana off their shoes and headed southwest.

In 1835 the couple arrived in Texas at an auspicious time in the future state's history. It is unknown where Sophia and Jesse first settled, but it mattered little. One day Jesse up and left his bride of two years and was never seen or heard from again. Why he left, whose fault it was, and other particulars of his departure are unknown. There is also a question of the legality of their marriage, or whether they were married at all. There is no record of a marriage license ever issued in their names.

Before he left, Jesse received a league of land from Mexican authorities, one of the last deeds authorized by that government. The drums of war were beating loudly. An overwhelming Mexican army led by the Napoleon of the West, Antonio López de Santa Anna, had bested the Alamo and its valiant defenders. Sophia and Jesse hardly had time to unpack their belongings, much less establish a homestead on their grant, which was located in today's Houston County.

Various accounts place Sophia on the San Jacinto battlefield on April 22, 1836, the day after the Texians defeated Mexican troops and officially declared the Republic of Texas, a proclamation that was tenuous but viable. Being in that area of Texas at the time, Sophia could well have been part of the Runaway Scrape, the flood of humanity that moved east as Santa Anna and his troops dogged their trail. Sophia's association with Sam Houston began at this time. She helped nurse him through his wounds and reportedly accompanied the Texas leader to New Orleans, where he underwent an operation on his shattered ankle.

Sophia apparently became something of a sutler herself. The merchandise she peddled required no inventory or wagon to move. There is no proof that Sophia sold *herself* to survive, but with employment opportunities for women being virtually nil, she could have turned to history's oldest profession to make ends meet. The profit would have been excellent, especially for someone who had Sophia's enticing looks and attractive figure. She remained in the Washington (later called Washington-on-the-Brazos) area for some time, and there is every reason to believe that the relationship between Houston and his former nurse was more than platonic. Sam was a known carouser in his day, and Sophia was the epitome of generosity.

Sophia was living near San Jacinto at the time of the short but important battle. Through some unknown route, she had hooked up with the sister of Holland Coffee and was living with her and her brother. Holland had been an early trader in Indian Territory (Oklahoma) and had established his headquarters in Fort Smith, Arkansas, in 1830. With the military buildup south of the Red River, which was encamped to ward off Indian attacks, he moved his trading post to a spot in today's Grayson County. In his enterprise was a young John Neely Bryan, who in the early 1840s began the settlement of what would become Dallas.

Holland had done well for himself in business, in the military (having attained the rank of colonel in the Texas army), and in politics. When he and Sophia met, he was the Fannin County representative in the Texas Congress. If there is such an emotion as love at first sight, Sophia and Holland experienced it. The fact that he had become a wealthy man through his various enterprises certainly did not turn her off.

Holland had arrived in Fort Smith via Kentucky and Tennessee. He formed a company with several partners and called the enterprise Coffee, Colville, and Company (Silas Cheek Colville was his major associate). While trading with the Indians, the respect of whom Holland received over time, he became acquainted with Sam Houston, who was living with the Cherokees. Holland was instrumental in arranging several Indian treaties. However, like many known personalities of the day, he was no fan of Houston. Among other actions, Representative Coffee voted against a proclamation expressing gratitude to Sam for his service as president of the Republic of Texas.

Holland's loyalties were never questioned; not so his ethics. Jim Bowie accused him of abetting raids into Texas from Indian Territory. In 1835 the Texas House Standing Committee on Indian Affairs recommended closing, or at least carefully watching, Coffee's Texas post. Holland challenged the charges in Houston, and the matter was dropped.

The matter of Sophia supposedly being married to someone else bothered neither of them one bit. They entered into the lifestyle of cohabitation without benefit of clergy. Their living arrangement probably would have attracted little comment had Holland not been a member of the august Texas Congress. Living in sin was inappropriate for one of the Republic's leaders.

To soothe the issue, on July 25, 1838, Sophia petitioned the Harris County District Court in Houston to grant her a divorce from the absentee Jesse Aughinbaugh. While this seems to indicate that Sophia considered herself legally attached to Jesse, nothing ever emerged to verify the fact. Since there was no defendant present to contest the divorce, the presiding judge, James W. Robinson, ruled on July 28, 1838, that the divorce would be enforced only if Jesse was not heard from by "the fifth Monday after the fourth Monday in October."

While the court was studying the divorce application, Sophia took up residence in Houston, seat of the district court. Holland did not accompany her; he was conducting negotiations between Indians and white colonists and attempting to settle some land claims. In 1838 Sophia earned income by operating a Houston boarding house for army recruits. Her good looks, flirtatious demeanor, and somewhat shady reputation led to whispers of Sophia earning extra income by furnishing extra services.

More pressing cases faced the district court than that of a divorce. Receiving no final resolution from the court, Sophia presented her case directly to the Third Texas Congress. The matter probably would have died in committee had it not been pushed by Representative Holland Coffee and the influential Sam Houston. Sophia received her divorce on January 19, 1839; she and Holland tied the knot in Washington four days later. Obviously, high power was exerted to get such a minor and personal decree passed when there was much more important business on the table.

Holland moved his new bride to his trading post near the Red River, a few miles northwest of present-day Denison (later the birthplace of Dwight D. Eisenhower). This was a new experience for Sophia. She quickly became accustomed to Indians patronizing the trading post from their camps north of the river. On rare occasions she reportedly had to barricade the store and fight off hostile Indians. And sometimes the post served as a bartering center for white captives, mostly women, brought in by Indians for trade. Another thing that required adjusting to was her neighbors: There were none for twenty-five miles, at a place called Warren's Trading House.

Holland and his partner, Silas, were doing well financially with their trading post. Business—and profit—boomed, though, when Preston Road and nearby Fort Johnson opened. Preston Road created a route from Indian Territory south to Central Texas. Livestock, commuters, and immigrants formed a constant flow of traffic and kept the Coffee-Colville cash drawer full. As for the fort, Holland's post supplied it with material, food, and other staples.

There is no indication that animosity reared its ugly head upon Holland's marriage to Sophia. Nevertheless, a year or so after the wedding, Coffee and Colville divided their property, each receiving equal distribution of all assets.

In 1842, a few years after settling down with Sophia, Holland began construction on what would become Glen Eden Plantation. The main house would never have received recognition by the Southern plantations in Louisiana, Mississippi, or other Old South locales. However, along the Red River of the mid-1800s, Glen Eden was a showcase to behold. Sophia held a housewarming that went on for several days. In time, Holland's landholdings amounted to around six thousand acres.

Mormons undertook construction of the new home. Led by Lyman Wright, the group had left Illinois and headed for Central Texas to set up a new commune. With the spacious new house and the affluence of her husband, Sophia became the great hostess of the region. Although it was remote and sparsely populated, there were several military installations around. Sophia reveled in the attention heaped on her by the handsome young military officers; the hostess often willingly returned their attention. Houston supposedly attended the grand opening of the plantation. Other visitors through the years included such prestigious figures as Ulysses S. Grant and Robert E. Lee.

Along with her lifestyle of the rich and famous, Sophia had a green thumb. She planted the first rose garden in Grayson County. Fruit trees covered acreage behind the palatial (for the time) home, and berries and grapes dotted the landscape. Visitors often brought seeds or plantings from far and wide. General Albert Sidney Johnston gave Sophia catalpa sprigs from California. Houston gave her magnolia sprigs, which Sophia planted in the front yard.

Holland spoke several Indian dialects. This talent made his services valuable not only in trade, but also in treaty confabs. He also was an outstanding guide and often directed or led travelers along dangerous and out-of-the-way trails. One expedition that he was tangled up in was the ill-fated Snively fiasco of 1843. Seeking retaliation for supposed indignities levied by Mexican troops, Jacob Snively led a group of some three hundred men (under semi-governmental sponsorship) toward Santa Fe, New Mexico, intending to take possession of cargo carried by Mexican wagons. Texans claimed part of the Santa Fe Trail as belonging to the Lone Star State. A brief scuffle ensued, and the Texians headed for home, in the process crossing Oklahoma to the Arkansas River. This put them on United States territory, and federal troops temporarily placed the adventurers under arrest.

Holland was spared the ultimate downfall and hardship, since he bailed out after a few miles down the trail. He wisely decided that he did not need to put his life on the line in such questionable undertakings. After all, his trading post on the Red River was probably the busiest commercial enterprise within miles.

Sophia was happy in her new life and reveled in the prestigious social position in which the community and travelers placed her. This period of elation came to an abrupt end in 1846, when Holland was killed in a duel. There was suspicion that the confrontation was brought on by Sophia's flirtations with either a soldier from one of the forts or, more than likely, with the grand patriarch of Texas, Sam Houston. In the area to serve as master of ceremonies at the dedication of the new courthouse in Sherman, Houston stayed with the Coffees. Holland's nephew by marriage, Charles A. Galloway, chided his aunt about her earlier relationship with Houston. Sophia took offense at Galloway's remarks, which she considered insulting.

Sophia asked her husband to defend her honor by rebuking the young man in a most severe manner. At first Holland refused to reproach Galloway, which only infuriated Sophia further. She called her husband a coward and continued to nag him about the blot Galloway had put on her reputation. Finally, on October 1, 1846, Holland challenged his nephew. The two met in the open in Preston for a fight to the death. Reportedly, Coffee was armed "with a bois d'arc stick, Bowie knife, single barrel pistol, six-shooter, and a double barrel shotgun loaded with buckshot." This arsenal did not prevent Galloway from fatally slicing up Coffee three times. The younger man walked away virtually unharmed.

The Grayson County District Court acquitted Galloway of murder. Members of the jury apparently respected both Coffee and Galloway and felt that neither of them wanted the duel to take place. In other words, those determining Galloway's fate decided that both parties were pressured into the duel, declaring that Galloway had acted in self-defense.

The result of the duel was that Sophia was now a widow and sole owner of Glen Eden Plantation. Holland's will left everything to his widow: "more than five thousand acres of land, nineteen slaves, herds of horses and cattle, his businesses . . . as well as Glen Eden." He also left her with substantial debt.

Sophia was not destined for widowhood very long. In late 1847 (or 1848 or 1853, depending on the source) she was in New Orleans to sell cotton, a trip she often made because she liked the social life of the French. There she met George N. Butt, a man who had left Norfolk, Virginia, with plans to join the Peters Colony, outside Dallas. The presence of the beguiling and bewitching Sophia changed his mind and his destination. (It was just as well. The Peters Colony failed to materialize, and most investors lost money on the endeavor.) Sophia and George married, and he returned with her to Glen Eden and became patriarch of the plantation.

Although Sophia presented George as her husband and the 1850 Grayson County census listed them as man and wife, there is no record of a marriage ceremony in either New Orleans or Texas. Still, a friend, Helen Morris Cummins of Sherman, stated that she attended the wedding reception at Glen Eden. Furthermore, a deed dated December 1847 bears the signature of Sophia Butt.

The legality of their union did not bother them, and Sophia was once again queen of the social scene. She entertained lavishly amid luxurious flora and fauna. Guests often brought her seedlings from both common and rare plants and grasses. She had a greenhouse that kept two slaves fully occupied year-round.

Some historians have asked whether the marriage, at least on Sophia's part, was more business than romance. After all, George either gave her cash or assumed the notes for $6,000, helping Sophia eliminate the financial burden left by her late husband. George also took responsibility for the education of Tennessee and Mary Jewell, two of Holland's nieces who resided at Glen Eden. For this contribution Sophia transferred to George 1,438 acres of land and three slaves.

Sophia and George were loyal Confederates, believing in the Southern cause. They sometimes went so far in their support as to indulge in some shanghaiing of recruits for the Confederate military. According to author Glenna Parker Middlebrooks, they more than once invited "transients and local men whom they regarded as slackers into their home and served 'refreshments' till the guests were in a state of mellow acquiescence.'" When the unfortunates came to their senses—each sporting a birdcage mouth and throbbing head—they found themselves dressed in Confederate gray and their signatures on enlistment forms.

Sophia's life, especially for the place and time, was one of splendid indulgence. But, again, gloom was just around the corner.

William Quantrill, a Confederate officer who lived to pillage, kill, and pretty much run rampant, decided that the Grayson County area would be a good place to quarter his troops. Locals were sympathetic to the South and at first welcomed Quantrill and his men. But the renegades could not leave well enough alone; they started treating their benefactors as prey. On Christmas Eve 1863, several of Quantrill's men, buoyed by John Barleycorn, crashed a dance at Ben Christian's Hotel in Sherman. One of the revelers cutting a rug was Sophia. The hooligans took potshots at the tassels hanging down from her hat and managed to shoot off a couple of them. Observers stated that Sophia "never stopped dancing."

George was found shot to death in February 1864. He did not agree with the renegade tactics of Quantrill's raiders and did not hesitate to speak out. After taking a load of cotton to the Sherman market, he was attacked from ambush and killed. Sophia, as well as many other residents, believed that Quantrill's men were guilty of the shooting. George's body was interred in the Sherman cemetery.

This was the straw that broke the camel's back. Evidence soon emerged proving that it was one of Quantrill's men who had killed George. Sophia, who was not without influence in the region, rallied Sherman residents to force Quantrill out of the area. The outrage became so vocal and angry that General Henry M. McCulloch, commander of

Confederate troops in Bonham, ordered the arrest of the bandit and his followers. The renegades escaped, however, by fleeing into Indian Territory. A few months later, Quantrill and his guerillas almost leveled Lawrence, Kansas, and killed some 150 people. Quantrill finally met his end during a raid in Kentucky. He was seriously wounded by Union troops and died in a prison hospital in June 1865.

After a respectable period of mourning, the widow Butt once more became hostess supreme.

Sophia gained a legendary footnote during the height of the Civil War that earned her a sobriquet in local recordings. A contingent of Confederate troops led by Colonel James Bourland stopped by Glen Eden on its way to Fort Washita, fifteen miles north in Indian Territory. Shortly after the Rebels departed Sophia's graceful renderings, a unit of Union soldiers arrived (some say they were Northern sympathizers). They were hunting for the Confederates, but Sophia, ever the enticing hostess, bid the men to dismount, refresh themselves, and partake of a splendid meal. When the soldiers had finished eating, Sophia gave them a key to her well-stocked wine cellar and invited them to indulge themselves.

Sophia later checked on her guests and, as she suspected, found them soused to the gills. She locked them in the cellar and headed north to warn the Confederates on the other side of the river about the Yankee soldiers. Here, as with much of the aura surrounding Sophia, facts become a bit muddled. One version has it that she mounted one of her mules and rode it across the frigid Red to warn the Rebels. By at least one account, Sophia's allies returned to Glen Eden and easily captured the inebriated enemy. Or maybe her absence gave the Confederates time to evacuate and live to fight another day. Regardless of the real story, history deemed Sophia the "Confederate Paul Revere" for her action.

Photograph of Sophia Porter taken shortly before she died in 1897

Either Union forces moved into the Grayson County area in greater number or Indian depredations became worse. Regardless of the reason, Sophia left Glen Eden and headed south to Waco, some 150 miles distant. A cautious lady, she realized she could not leave cash behind; it would not be there when she returned. So the enterprising woman placed gold coins in the bottoms of buckets, filled the containers with hot tar, hung them underneath her wagon, and took off.

It was in Waco that Sophia met her fourth and last husband. Still attractive, she captivated James Porter, a widower and former judge from Independence, Missouri. They were married on August 2, 1865, by Rufus C. Burleson, president of Baylor College (now University). Soon after, the newlyweds returned to Glen Eden.

Maybe some outside influence took over Sophia's soul. Or perhaps she gained some perspective on the life she had led, for religion suddenly took hold of the woman some locals considered rather bawdy. Author Sherrie S. McLeRoy reports that "At a camp meeting one night . . . she ran down the aisle in an orange satin dress and threw herself at the feet of the Reverend John Witherspoon Pettigrew McKenzie, a Methodist minister." The reverend was aware of Sophia's history, real or imagined, and refused to accept her into the congregation. "He informed her . . . that she would have to do good deeds for twelve years before he'd let her into his church. And he wasn't hopeful even then, for 'the sun, the moon, and the stars' were all against her becoming a Christian."

The First Methodist Church of Sherman, pastored by the Reverend J. M. Binkley, had no such qualms. Binkley believed that the source of much area gossip could be redeemed and accepted her into his congregation. The minister's faith was well vested, and he and Sophia were friends for life. She served the church well and supported several charities, among them the Rescue Home of Dallas for "fallen women" and Southwestern University in Georgetown.

Here again that old nagging foible of a large question mark enters the story. Sophia's sudden turnaround in moral attitude and values might have been influenced more by her new husband than another other pressure or awakening. Upon his moving to Glen Eden with Sophia, the judge immediately stepped into local civic affairs. He helped establish a Methodist Church and Sunday school; Sophia joined in the endeavors alongside him.

While the plantation continued to host social gatherings, no longer did the soirees last for days on end. It is reported that "The wine cellar was emptied of its liquors, and without anyone quite knowing how it came about, Glen Eden became the Porter House."

James died of natural causes on September 10, 1886, twenty-one years after his marriage to Sophia. Their union was her longest marital connection by far and from all indications, the happiest. Sophia interred James in nearby Preston under a marble tombstone that she had engraved, HE MADE HOME HAPPY.

James's death pushed Sophia into a melancholy mood. At age seventy-one she realized that playing the hostess role as she might, she was no longer an enticement to her male guests. They looked aside, to younger and more attractive women. Sophia was not aging gracefully. Belle Evans, a friend of long standing, moved to Glen Eden at Sophia's behest and became a benevolent Svengali for her friend. The two women often took shopping trips together, searching out fashions that might restore the beauty Sophia once enjoyed so much.

This was an exercise in futility. Frontier life in Texas was demanding and harsh, and regardless of how much money Sophia had at her disposal, little could be done to forestall the ravages of time and the inevitable signs of age brought on by the elements. Belle even applied hair dye on a weekly basis in an attempt to bring back the black luster that had once added to Sophia's attractiveness. Neither woman seemed to realize that the ebony sheen only emphasized the wrinkles in Sophia's face and made her skin tone look even harsher.

Soon Sophia became cantankerous. She invoked fear in her servants, though they always tried to please her. McLeRoy relates that Sophia had Belle "check the servants' mouths to make sure they weren't stealing fruit from her prize berry vines." It was a sign that her mind was slipping.

Sophia remained at Glen Eden, where she spent her remaining years tending to her plants and flowers, the seedlings of which represented various sections of the United States, few being native to the area. Eleven years after James Porter had breathed his last, Sophia succumbed to death on August 27, 1897, following a short illness. Reverend Binkley was with her in her final moments and conducted the eulogy at her beloved Glen Eden. She was interred next to James in the Preston Cemetery.

Death seems to have a humanizing effect on those who were reviled in life. Sophia's past was overlooked, and in noting her death, the local newspaper declared her an "aged saint with a sweet spirit." It is doubtful that many of her acquaintances of an earlier generation would have been so generous in their praise. Yet Sophia could not have cared less what people thought about her. Four black horses carried the deceased to the gravesite. Her final raiment reportedly consisted of a pink satin dress trimmed in black lace. Sophia was eighty-one years old at the time of her demise.

Sophia willed Glen Eden to her nephew, J. W. Williams, and a friend, Mary Elizabeth Jewell Mosely. Planners attempted to preserve the main house that had served as Sophia's showcase, entertainment palace, and scene of her idyllic trysts. When plans were made to flood the area for Lake Texoma, interested parties disassembled the house, numbered each piece, and set the artifacts aside for later restoration.

Unaware of the significance of the lumber, soldiers camped in the area one frigid night burned the wood for heat.

Sophia's body lies in a small plot of land near the locale of her former beloved plantation. On one side of her is the grave of Holland Coffee, on the other that of James Porter. Her tombstone bears the engraving I KNOW THAT MY REDEEMER LIVETH. Sophia had no children but raised two nieces of Holland. Their whereabouts were lost in the mist of time.

And so passed from the stage of life another of those controversial yet unique individuals who make history so interesting. Sophia Porter was by no means a solo act in Texas in the 1800s. The territory turned republic turned state foisted many women to the forefront who were strong, took their own paths, and defied social convention every waking moment. They added spice to the recipe of life.

Mollie Bailey

SHE PLAYED THE CENTER RING

In 1871 Connecticut-born Phineus Taylor Barnum, following many years in exhibitive show business, started a circus that later would be coined "the Greatest Show on Earth." James A. Bailey became a partner some years later. In 1907 the five Ringling brothers, who had been traveling the circuit with their own circus, bought the Barnum and Bailey enterprise. The two outfits traveled under separate billings until 1919, when they became one, the Ringling Brothers and Barnum & Bailey Circus. Although the Ringlings sold the operation in 1967, the new owners were wise enough to keep the legendary name.

At the same time that Barnum & Bailey was making a name for itself playing in large cities, a smaller circus was showing up in venues around Texas. Bailey's Circus (no relation to James A., who was born McGuiness but took the surname of his benefactor, Fred Harrison Bailey), in its own way, was just as successful as its larger competitor. Also, like P. T. Barnum's stroke of genius, Bailey's Circus was an emergence, something that developed over a period of time. It started as a husband-and-wife effort, but the wife—"Aunt" Mollie Bailey—eventually took over full operation of the circus. Mollie was another of those unique, strong, independent, and self-sustaining women who roamed Texas in the 1800s.

Mollie Arline Kirkland is believed to have been born November 2, 1844, on a plantation near Mobile, Alabama. Had the wishes of her parents (William and Mary) prevailed, Mollie would have grown up to be mistress of the plantation and then, after marriage, become the matriarch of her well-to-do husband's estate. The only problem was that Mollie's plans and those of her father did not match. Her differing view of the future should have been apparent early in her life, as well as the lives of her siblings. Mollie had early theatrical inclinations and led her siblings in the same direction.

By age twelve, Mollie was described as a "beautiful young girl" with a "gypsy-like appearance, dark hair, flashing black eyes, and a vivacious manner . . . a graceful, charming young lady, a belle of the day." Mollie pursued her "female deportment" education at a ladies school at Tuscaloosa, southwest of Birmingham. She stayed at the school for two years and then returned home to the family plantation for vacation.

In life there is often an event, a moment, or a person that changes the course of that life forever. It was at age fourteen, while home from school, that Mollie met the person who would change her life. The man was Gus Bailey, a circus bandleader and coronet player and the son of a circus owner. Mollie fell head over heels for the traveling troubadour, but when she confessed her love to her father, he forbade any marriage between the two. He had higher aspirations for his daughter than some traveling musician.

Born with a will of her own, a trait that would prove to be a winning asset later in life, Mollie disregarded her father's warning. On March 21, 1858, she and Gus married. The couple left the area soon after and celebrated their honeymoon on the road with the circus. Mollie attempted on at least two occasions to make peace with her father. He was not a forgiving soul and eventually disinherited her. If this familial setback disturbed Mollie, she never let on, and it certainly did nothing to lessen the happiness and success that life afforded her and that she made for herself.

Ambitious, determined, and intelligent, Mollie convinced her husband that they should form their own show and separate themselves from his father's circus. Gus agreed, but they had limited financial resources and little, if any, traveling gear. Innately honest, Mollie did veer from the straight and narrow—she sneaked back to the family plantation one night and purloined some horses and wagons from her father's inventory.

The horses and wagons did not carry circus equipment. Rather, the Bailey Family Troupe, as the operation became known, was a vaudeville act that traveled throughout Alabama, Arkansas, and Mississippi, performing wherever they could find an audience. The troupe presented a talented family to the audience. Gus was an all-around performer: a comedian, leading man in skits, fiddler, and when not on stage, the leader of the band. Alfred, Gus's brother, was a musician and a contortionist, always a big draw in small, rural communities. Fannie Kirkland, Mollie's half-sister, was an actress and a dancer. As for Mollie, she was Gus's counterpart in the lead arena. She served as female star, solo singer, and organ player. Fannie and Alfred stayed with Mollie and Gus for many years.

On May 21, 1861, just weeks after the outbreak of the Civil War, Gus enlisted in the Confederate army in Selma, Alabama. His first assignment was to the Forty-Fourth Alabama Infantry. About a year and a half later, he transferred to Company Thirteen of the Arkansas Infantry. This unit was part of Hood's Texas Brigade. The Bailey trek to the West had offically begun. Gus commanded the Third Arkansas Band and played with a group of musicians and actors known as Hood's Minstrels.

An accomplished musician, Gus was apparently adept at composing music as well. It was during the Civil War that he penned "The Old Grey Mare, She Ain't What She Used to Be," a ditty still familiar to older generations today. The song supposedly related to an actual horse that nearly died after consuming green corn but got better with the help of medicine. A friend of Gus's put the words to music; the piece became a military march and, much later, the official song of the 1928 Democratic National Convention, held in Houston.

Mollie stepped up to do her part in the war effort. She had recently given birth to the first of nine children, Dixie, whom she left with friends in Richmond, Virginia. Initially, Mollie served as a nurse in a field hospital or wherever she was needed. When the troops went into winter quarters, she and Fannie performed with Hood's Minstrels, singing and dancing to entertain the soldiers. Mollie did not stop with nursing and entertaining. She donned the mantle of a Confederate spy on more than one occasion. Her expertise as a thespian, coupled with nerves of steel, served her well in such times.

Several women performed as spies during the Civil War. They did have some advantages. If captured, their penalty would be prison instead of a firing squad. Too, the female persona itself often served to deflect suspicion. This was a tremendous asset toward accomplishing the mission.

Mollie's acting ability served her especially well on one of the spy forays. Dressed in an old woman's garments and wearing makeup that made her face appear years older than she really was, Mollie was able not only to penetrate the Union pickets, but also to remain among enemy forces for a time. She portrayed an elderly woman doling out cookies to the Yankee soldiers. Virtually invisible to the soldiers, Mollie was able to gather desired information and return to the Confederate camp.

Lacking the elements of a spy mission, Mollie once undertook a perilous trip through enemy lines for a more humane reason. Being a nurse, she knew of shortages of medicine, including quinine. She hoped to deliver some to the soldiers of the Third Arkansas unit, but to reach them, she would have to travel through risky territory. Mollie devised a plan. She had the quinine powder wrapped in small bags, then hid the packets in her pompadour hairstyle. It worked perfectly. Mollie made the round-trip safely, and her supplies relieved the pain of many soldiers. The plan worked so brilliantly that one officer praised Mollie's deed like so: "Depend on a woman to think up a good scheme."

The nation's most divisive and devastating conflict ended in April 1865. Much of the country, especially the South, was destitute, void of both property and money. The Baileys were no different. And like many other veterans, Gus had contracted some type of respiratory illness, probably consumption (tuberculosis) from the cold, damp nights on the ground in Arkansas. On top of all this, he and Mollie now had three young daughters to care for. In desperation the Baileys hooked up with a showboat group not particularly to their liking. The Bailey family continued to grow with the addition of four sons.

The Baileys tired of the showboat tour and quit to form the Bailey Concert Company. They continued with their touring preferences: small towns and rural areas of the South. The family was a self-sustained, talented group. According to author Martha Hartzog, "Mollie played the organ, Gus the fiddle, the older boys sang, and they had a few dancing acts."

The concert company slowly evolved into essentially a circus, although it was not yet known by that designation. The Baileys moved from site to site by wagon and pitched tents for entertaining. Their offerings consisted of trapeze high flyers, dancing and musical presentations, comedy, sideshows, and a band. It was a family show

Courtesy of Western History Collections, University of Oklahoma

Mollie Bailey and her favorite horse and buggy

and appealed to the rural ethic the Baileys preferred. Everything was aboveboard; there were no crooked goings-on or other shenanigans to concern the audience. Old and young, male and female, a joyous time was had by all.

Needing a base to which they could return during the off-season, the Baileys bought a home in Prescott, Arkansas, in the southwestern part of the state. Gus's debilitating illness began to take its toll. As a result, operation of the family business fell squarely on Mollie's more-than-capable shoulders. All things considered, she was probably the main character in the family saga anyway.

It was 1876, and by this time in her life, Mollie's enticing figure had morphed somewhat, leaving her "a short, rounded figure of a woman, with a small waist and a positive walk," according to Hartzog. "Well dressed in dark, rich materials, her skirt billowed as she walked, her eyes sparkled, and her lips gave 'mother wit.'" Serving on the front line during the Civil War, giving birth to nine children and traveling almost constantly with her family business should have taken much out of Mollie mentally. It is a tribute to her fortitude and determination that very little of her personality was altered over the years.

The purchase of a home in Prescott placed the Baileys even closer to their real destination. For some time Mollie and Gus had wanted to move their entertainment enterprise to Texas, tempted by stories of numerous settlers heading for the large open spaces of the Lone Star State. Although the Civil War deterred the Baileys from making the move, their service with Hood's Texas Brigade served to whet their appetite for the land on the western side of the Red River.

Their dream bore fruit in 1885. The Baileys bought a home in Dallas, at South Prescott and Young Streets, which would serve as their winter quarters. Two years after moving to Texas, the Bailey production became a circus in every sense of the word, from the clowns to acts performed in the rings. Proud of its new home and revamped enterprise, the Bailey Circus adopted the motto "A Texas Show for Texas People." As a reflection of the times, three flags flew from the three poles that supported the circus tent: the Stars and Stripes of the United States, the Lone Star of the Republic of Texas, and the Confederate Stars and Bars. All loyalties were covered.

Mollie and Gus followed their established routine of playing only small venues. This was a wise plan for several reasons: They did not have to compete with larger, more established circuses; advertising expenses were held to a minimum; and what the Baileys missed in monetary benefits they made up for in audience loyalty. Farmers, small-town merchants, schoolkids, and townspeople who were more rural than urban flocked to see the Bailey Circus every year that it came to their area. The performers always pleased the viewers and left them anticipating the show's return the following year.

Although not subject to the rigidity and formality necessary for playing in New York, Philadelphia, or Chicago, the Bailey Circus still had to map out routes, stops, and the myriad other problems that go into such an operation as a circus. The tour generally left Dallas in the spring, traveled through East Texas and then on to South Texas, and turned north after that, stopping at sites in the Dallas area. From there, the circus wended its way northwest through West Texas and the Panhandle, finally returning to Dallas in December for its winter hibernation.

Mollie, ever the shrewd entrepreneur, purchased lots in the most frequented towns on the circus's schedule. This was to avoid the high taxes placed on entertainment outlets of the day. When the circus was away from the area, she would let the communities use the land as playing fields, picnic grounds, or whatever civic activity was deemed appropriate. When the site was no longer on the circus route, Mollie usually deeded the land back to the town.

The Bailey Circus was successful, and Mollie put much of her profit into charitable endeavors. As Barbara Barton writes in her article, "Good Golly, Miss Molly," she not only contributed to Confederate memorials, but some "fifty congregations in Texas were helped to own their church buildings through her generosity." She always granted free entry to the circus for war veterans, regardless of which color uniform they had worn. Mollie also saw to it that the poorer children of the area received passes to the performances.

Despite this open-door policy, Mollie was once surprised by some unexpected visitors to her circus, as Martha Hartzog relates in *Legendary Ladies of Texas*. Although the Indian population had been largely contained by this time, there were renegade bands roaming the countryside. The circus had stopped for the night in the country, between two towns, and the wagons were circled, as was customary.

The troupe was busy preparing supper when Mollie saw shadows outside the wagon perimeter. She took a pistol that had been her companion since the war and fired into the air. Nothing happened. Suddenly, getting an inspiration, Mollie began hitting the circus's large drum. As the figures fled from the scene, they were identified as Indians.

Hartzog continues, "When the circus was in Quanah, Texas, Mollie told the story to Quanah Parker, famous Indian chief. He enjoyed it immensely and each year when the show came to town, he would ask Mollie to tell it again, doubling up in laughter."

Ill health finally caught up with Gus in 1890 and forced him to retire to Blum; he passed away in 1896. For years people had referred to the road show as "the Mollie A. Bailey Show;" now it became fact. It was around this time that she acquired the moniker "Aunt Mollie." The circus was at its zenith in popularity and boasted "thirty-one wagons, 170 head of stock, twenty-one trained ponies, and a collection of working animals," according to Hartzog. Elephants and camels became part of the menagerie in 1902.

The general operation of the circus followed the same procedure at each event: According to Hartzog, "Mollie always stood at the entrance. . . . With a blast of the trumpet, the show began. In tumbled the clowns. There were at least six and one of them always dressed as a woman. With a more innocent motive than possible today, 'she' flirted with whatever dignitary was in the crowd."

The opening ceremonies continued to enthrall the audience. Birda, the Bailey's youngest daughter, rode in on a black horse with Shetland ponies bringing up the rear. There were dog and pig acts and the proverbial, for the time, clown chased by an Indian. Allie and Brad, two of the Bailey boys, performed wire-walking acts.

Mollie, among her other accomplishments, is credited with showing the first motion picture in Texas. The film was shown in a smaller tent adjacent to the main tent, and its subject was the sinking of the battleship *Maine* in Havana Harbor. The blast took place on February 15, 1898, and was one of the events that precipitated the Spanish-American War.

Mollie took her show to county fairs, and schools dismissed students for half a day to enjoy the rides and thrill of the daredevil performers. Veterans of the Civil War timed their reunions around Mollie's scheduled appearance, and each veteran made a point of passing by and shaking hands with her. Although a Southern sympathizer during the war, she treated all veterans —Blue and Gray—equally. Mollie may have been hesitant about relating her wartime deeds, but the old veterans were not, and they talked about her serving as a spy and nurse.

People off the street as well as from the statehouse viewed the performances. It was even reported that Texas governor James Stephen Hogg presented Mollie with a gold-mounted wild boar's tooth (from a boar he had shot) with her name inscribed on it; she wore it as a brooch.

Mollie was determined that her circus would be family oriented and good, clean fun for all. Her brother-in-law, Alfred Bailey, was responsible for keeping the circus on a "Sunday School" track. Under this aegis, no drinking on the premises was tolerated, no cursing by the employees, and no duping the customers. Employees were to be at top speed at all times when the circus was open. The fear of injury or death hung over the operation like an albatross.

Mollie was a hands-on owner, which would prove to be a detriment down the road. She oversaw all aspects of the circus operation, from advertisement to wagons, from performers to animals. And something that certainly endeared her to employees and suppliers alike was her practice of always paying cash. As Hartzog notes, she carried "a big dark purse as she went along."

In 1906 the Bailey Circus lost much of its character and many of its small venues. That was the year Mollie changed the mode of transportation from wagons to the more economical and speedier trains. Not content with being simply a passenger on the rails, she bought two Pullman cars and a parlor car for herself. In the latter she socialized with many well-known Texas figures of the day, including governors Branch Colquitt and James Hogg, as well as the likes of legislators Joseph Bailey (no relation) and Morris Sheppard. Former members of Hood's Texas Brigade were always welcome to her plush accommodations, where reminiscences flowed freely and at length.

It was also in 1906 that Mollie married A. H. "Blackie" Hardesty. The age of her second husband is unknown, but he was much younger than sixty-two-year-old Mollie. Blackie assumed limited managerial control of the circus, with Mollie always pulling the strings. He lost his personal identity when people began referring to him as Blackie Bailey, apparently at Mollie's insistence.

Birda became ill in 1917, and Mollie moved to Houston to take care of her. Mollie never lost control of the circus, however, keeping in daily contact through telephone calls, telegrams, and mail. Birda died in September 1917, but Mollie did not return to the circus. The following year she fell and broke her hip. For reasons undetermined at the time, she was unable to recover. She died from other causes on October 2 of that year and was buried in Hollywood Cemetery in Houston. The energetic entrepreneur was eulogized thusly: "It is said that her heart did not stop beating for two hours after her death."

The four Bailey boys—Allie, Brad, Eugene, and A. K.—continued with the circus for a while but did not have their mother's intensity or ability. The boys wandered off in other directions, and with no one trained to manage—one of Mollie's few failings—the circus soon folded. Although Blackie had assumed the position of manager, he never really had absolute control, training, or power. He became a bus driver, living in Baytown and driving a route between Houston and Goose Creek, a community on Galveston Bay, southeast of Houston. Blackie died in 1937; his place of interment is unknown.

About thirty years after Mollie's enterprise closed for good, the better-known and much larger Ringling Brothers and Barnum & Bailey Circus lowered its tent for the last time, on July 16, 1956. After it came under new management, performances moved to indoor arenas, civic centers, and the like. The days of sawdust on the ground were over. Another symbol of America faded away.

Author Martha Hartzog, mentioned above, provides this telling example of how people in the country and rural areas felt about Mollie and her circus: "In 1952, Mrs. J. C. Byers of Coolidge, Texas, wrote a letter to the editor of *Texas Parade* describing with fondness the devotion her husband and son had given to Mollie Bailey many years before. When she asked her husband why he persisted in seeing the same old show over and over, he replied, 'Why it's just like turning down your own folks to turn her down. She is every thing a show should be— clean, wholesome, no shin games. She's . . . well, she's Mollie Bailey, and I'm going to her show as long as she comes over the road.'"

That is a great memorial for anyone. It certainly disproves the assertion that history remembers only naughty women.

6

Bass Outlaw

RANGER LITTLE WOLF

The Texas mystique is based on many factors: land, people, history, oil, cattle, and cowboys, to list a few. No factor serves the state's ego, fiction, and fact better than the Texas Rangers. This institution of daring and honesty has not always lived up to its image—but few institutions do. The Ranger service was used for political gain, almost driven to extinction, abolished, and finally established into the exceptional law enforcement agency it is today, although its prestige and power have waned.

The official date of birth of the Rangers has always drawn debate. In 1823 Stephen F. Austin, the Father of Texas, called for ten men to serve as "ranging" officers. There is no record that such a force ever officially came into being. Three years later, Austin once again called for a ranging force to man six militia districts. In 1835 the Texas Rangers gained legality by the Consultation (the governing body at the time of Texas's thrust into independence). The stated purpose of the Rangers was to fight Indians and repel possible Mexican raids from the west. Later, as Texas emerged into statehood, the charges increased to include taking on outlaw bands, rustlers, and riots.

Many men honored themselves in service as Rangers. Two even became governors of the state (Peter Bell and Lawrence Sullivan Ross), though most remained in the field of law enforcement. The Ranger honor roll of fame is replete with names of men who did themselves well, among them John "Jack" Coffee Hays, John R. Hughes, and Frank A. Hamer Jr.

Hays (the namesake of Hays County) was a Ranger leader during the Mexican-American War, the only time the force ever became involved in foreign conflict. Shortly after the war, Hays moved to California; due to his background, he was appointed sheriff of San Francisco County. He served in that position for four years, until President Franklin Pierce appointed him surveyor general of California. In 1853 Hays and five friends paid $10,000 for a plot of land across the bay from San Francisco and Hays laid out the city that is known today as Oakland. He died in 1883 near Piedmont, California. His life as a Ranger, and his subsequent California exploits, are the stuff of which motion pictures are made.

Hughes wore a Ranger badge for twenty-eight years, from 1887 to 1915. He was a solemn man who preferred not to wear a gun, although he strapped one on when necessary while covering the untamed Pecos region of Texas. Hughes's place in glory was assured when Zane Grey wrote a novel of the West titled *The Lone Star Ranger*, using Hughes as the model for his hero. From this developed the fabled Lone Ranger character.

Hamer Jr., who had twenty-three scars from gunshot wounds and sixteen bullets in his body when he died in his sleep in 1955, is best remembered for an incident that took place while he was off duty. On May 23, 1934, he and some other lawmen set up a roadblock on a rural Louisiana road and killed two of the most infamous gangsters in American history: Bonnie Parker and Clyde Barrow.

These three men helped establish the legendary Ranger model of bravado, stature, and courage, as represented in the oft-repeated yarn about the small town in Texas rife with riot. The town pleaded to the governor for assistance. The chief executive sent help, but when city fathers met the train, they were staggered to see only one man step down.

"You mean the governor sent only *one* Ranger?" they asked.

"Well, you have only one riot, don't you?" was the famous reply.

And yet all agencies have an occasional bad apple—a member of the organization who never fits in, the one who fails to measure up to the standards expected of the group. The Rangers would long rue the day they acquired their misfit.

One day in 1885, a Georgian by the unlikely name of Bass Outlaw meandered into Ranger headquarters at Camp Wood, Real County, about eight miles west of San Antonio. He wanted to enlist. Captain Frank Jones scrutinized the almost pathetic example of manhood slouching in front of him: Only five-foot-four, Bass was thin, pale, and sported an odd mustache. Jones questioned the man's name but was assured by the applicant that it was legal and given him by his parents back in Georgia.

It is possible that Bass's real name was Sebastian Lamar Outlaw. If this is true, it is easy to understand why he changed it once he reached Texas and decided to become a lawman. Some of Bass's fellow Rangers believed that he fled Georgia to escape a murder charge. Bass evidently followed the GTT (Gone to Texas) trail.

Bass was enlisted in 1885 at age thirty, not so much because he looked like a sound prospect—which he did not—but because recruits were hard to come by. This was one of those times when the old adage of still water running deep proved to be most profound. Bass was a loner, never volunteering anything about his past, never asking anyone about theirs. A moody, sullen, often cantankerous individual, he was pretty much left to his own company. However, he possessed the nerve and derring-do that the Rangers required in those days on a wild and unsettled frontier.

Modern-day psychologists have stated that the greatest trauma a law enforcement official can experience is having to kill someone. The same was no doubt true of the frontier Texas Rangers. Except for in a few early years of the twentieth century along the Texas-Mexico border, Rangers killed only when they had to, preferring to take their quarry alive. Bass Outlaw proved from the beginning that he was not cut from the same strands of rawhide.

Bass seemed to enjoy the opportunity as much as the actuality of killing, and wearing the badge of a Texas Ranger made it legal. One Christmas Eve, Bass was one of a quartet of Rangers hiding along a dark and lonely road, awaiting the passing of two desperadoes; joining him were Hughes, Ira Aten, and deputy sheriff Will Terry. The lawmen learned that the two rustlers would be traveling to Barksdale, Edwards County, to join in holiday festivities. Outlaw and his compadres secreted themselves outside the small community of Vance, in Real County, across the county line from Barksdale.

When the outlaws—Will and Alvin Odle—rode into the trap, the Rangers fired warning shots with their revolvers and rifles. The bandits made the mistake of returning fire, whereupon they were soon lying facedown on the cold December ground. Bass volunteered to bury the deceased in a temporary grave until relatives could come and give them a decent burial. When his cohorts had departed, Bass crouched over the dead men and attempted to determine where *his* shots had entered the lifeless bodies by examining the bullet holes with his fingers.

While the Rangers would have preferred gentlemanly types for its ranks, such was not always possible. The danger, long hours, low

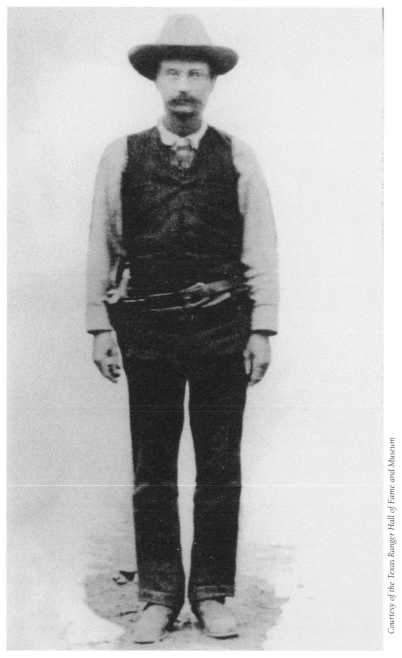

Bass Outlaw, old-time Texas Ranger, and all-around bad man, who was killed by Selman

pay, and absence of any semblance of home life deterred many solid citizens from offering their services. Despite the drawbacks, to fill the ranks Ranger authorities seldom had to stoop as low as they did to take in Bass Outlaw. He was more a saloon player, gambler, and whiskey drinker who took most of his nourishment from a bottle (regardless of brand or quality) and acquired his pleasures from the women usually found in saloons of the day. Though small in stature, he feared no man on this earth; indeed, with his drunken temper, most men feared him and his accuracy with a pistol.

Some of Bass's contemporaries inexplicably considered him the epitome of Southern gentility and even looked on him as a well-educated man and exceptionally polite. Those personal traits took a 180-degree turn when Bass overindulged in wild spirits. People would even pull children off the streets when he was in one of his drunken stupors.

It was alcohol that presumably drew Bass about seven miles from Ranger headquarters one day, to a still run by a man named Potter. Making himself absent without leave, Bass mounted his horse and headed for the still. Upon his arrival he saw two Mexicans drinking moonshine and Potter standing nearby. Bass recognized the two men from wanted posters back at the Ranger station. When they greeted him in broken English, Bass drew his pistol and killed them both on the spot. It was his reaction that earned him the nickname that was to stick with him until his death, one that he relished and never challenged.

Aten, who had been inspired to become a Texas Ranger after witnessing the shooting of notorious criminal Sam Bass, was a member of the same company as Outlaw. Aten was sent to bring the AWOL Bass back to headquarters for a reaming out. Captain Jones had on several occasions decided to fire the errant lawman but each time was persuaded to do otherwise by some heroic deed by the malcontent. This time would be no different. How could he sack someone who had just rid the county of two bandits?

Aten stated that when he came upon the scene, "Bass was looking at those two like a little wolf that's just made a jump kill on a calf. I thought he was gonna fly right out of the saddle and tear those corpses apart." From that day forward, Bass Outlaw was known as Little Wolf, seldom in a complimentary sense.

Perhaps the most profound observation ever made about Bass came from fellow Ranger John Hughes. It was after one of Bass's more sullen moods had overtaken him and he had ridden off, heading for the nearest saloon and a night of pleasure. Standing with Captain Jones and watching Bass depart, Hughes commented, "Captain, one of these days Bass Outlaw will kill a Ranger." Whether he realized it or not, Hughes had the gift of insight.

But other adventures transpired before that came to pass. In those days Rangers could be furloughed for a time to earn extra money doing various jobs that usually called on their ability with firearms. Once, Fronteriza, an American silver mining company operating in Coahuila, Mexico, hired Bass, along with fellow Rangers Hughes and Walter Durbin, to serve as guards. Bill Grady, Captain Jones's brother-in-law, worked at the mine and requested Ranger assistance. The work site was some eighty miles south of the Rio Grande.

Northern Mexico, in particular the area covered by the guards, is mountainous terrain. In episodes reminiscent of scenes from *Butch Cassidy and the Sundance Kid,* Bass and his fellow guards put to rest many bandits and robbers who took advantage of the landscape to ambush wagons hauling silver from the mine to nearby towns.

Surprisingly, Bass showed great improvement during part of his tenure with Fronteriza. His drinking eased to an acceptable level, his pockets bulged with high wages, and he even avoided the many women available in the cantinas. Alas, such respite was not to last. One night, while sitting in their small cabin, Hughes and Durbin heard gunshots. They ran outside and rushed in the direction of the local store. Peering through a window, they saw Bass, reeling from drink and waving a pistol. Standing on the opposite side of the room were several Mexican employees of the mine, their hands held high, fear etched on their faces. At Bass's feet was another Mexican, also a mine employee. The body was motionless, and blood oozed from bullet holes.

Knowing that if they rushed through the door Bass would just as likely turn on them and put bullets in their heads, Hughes and Durbin let caution be their guide. Before the two decided what to do, Bass started edging toward the door, warning the occupants of the store not to follow him. When he stepped outside Hughes and Durbin grabbed him and wrestled the pistol from his hand. Little Wolf, drunk or sober, was no man to tangle with and was more than even these bigger, stronger men could handle. Hughes used Bass's own gun to quiet the troublemaker, laying the barrel across his head. They hurried to their cabin, dragging Bass with them. Once inside they barricaded the door with a table, chairs, and anything else they could find in the room. They feared that they would have to take on the entire mining camp as repayment for Bass's foolhardy act.

It soon appeared as though the Rangers' fear would materialize. When Hughes looked out the window, he saw five miners walking toward the cabin. He took a carbine and stepped outside; Durbin covered him from inside by ramming his rifle through a window. As it turned out, their worry was for naught. It seems the man Bass killed was so disliked by the other miners, they considered it a blessing that the gringo had rid them of such a nuisance. Once again, Bass's luck held. In his own defense, Bass later said that the dead miner had pulled a knife on him.

Despite his reputation and being detested by most of his fellow Rangers, Bass was promoted back in Texas when the unit's sergeant, a man named Fusselman, was killed in a battle with Mexican bandits near El Paso. Bass received his stripes simply because Captain Jones felt he had earned them. Too, Jones hoped the added responsibility would cause Bass to clean up his act. Amazingly, for a time it did seem to steer Bass on a straighter path. But the straight and narrow was a road Little Wolf found extremely difficult to travel, at least for any length of time.

In 1893, after the Ranger company had moved to Alpine, about two hundred remote miles southeast of El Paso, Bass was placed in charge of the unit while Captain Jones was away on business. One day, after tilting the redeye once too often, Bass left the compound with no one in command and joined a poker game with a former Ranger, Abe Anglin, in the Buckhorn Saloon in Alpine. Bass was bested in the game by Anglin, but in his drunken stupor he started walking off with the winnings. Anglin challenged him.

Knowing what would happen were matters allowed to continue, the bartender sent an urgent plea for the sheriff. Only a split second before Bass and Anglin were ready to empty their holsters, Alpine sheriff Jim Gillett, another former Ranger, entered the saloon. Gillett grabbed Bass and pulled him outside. The sheriff managed to settle matters before there was any gunfire.

Upon returning to Alpine, Jones learned of Bass's carrying on. The captain was furious and fired the Ranger on the spot, paying him off and ordering him out of camp.

From that day forward, until he drew his last breath, Bass held a grudge against the Rangers. His bone of contention was at first with Gillett, because he thought the sheriff had ratted to Jones. Soon, through an intermediary, Bass learned that the lawman had not reported his behavior in the saloon. Gillett was spared; he was not the Ranger that Bass was destined to kill.

For a while after being pink-slipped, Bass prospected for gold, following one of the proverbial tales about hidden treasure somewhere in the West. His pot of riches proved to be nonexistent. There is speculation that he was not really after gold, that silver was his target. While still a member of Jones's company, Bass had been in on the chase of outlaws who had robbed a train near Sanderson, in Terrell County, and reputedly made off with between $50,000 and $60,000. The dusty wayside of Sanderson, another of those West Texas "garden spots" a few miles from the Mexican border, was frequent host to rustlers, gunmen, and bandits. Roy Bean, the famous "Law West of the Pecos," once operated a saloon there, and another drinking establishment, the Old Cottage Bar, held sway with a wild reputation in those early days.

After being alerted to the robbery, Jones and his men took off in pursuit. They lost the outlaws near the Rio Grande and gave up the chase, at least for the moment. The lawmen undertook additional expeditions to find the robbers, but to no avail. They finally located their quarry camped on the Rio Grande near the eastern entrance to what is now rugged Big Bend National Park. The robbers spotted the Rangers and hit their saddles. The chase lasted for several days, finally ending some 140 miles east, near present-day Ozona, Crockett County.

There were four men in the gang. Three of them were captured; their leader was shot but managed to ride into a thicket of mesquite, where he put a gun to his head. When things settled down, it was discovered that the gang was using sacks that once held money from the train robbery to carry coffee and sugar, but none of the desperadoes had much cash on his person. Speculation had it that they buried the loot near their camp on the Rio Grande. This, in view of some, was Bass's real prospecting goal. The silver—if there ever was such a treasure—was never found.

With another failure behind him, Little Wolf turned to the one profession he was good at, that of lawman. U. S. Marshal Dick Ware, El Paso, took Bass on as a deputy. Ware was an ex-Ranger and still celebrated the notoriety he had gained from his part in ending desperado Sam Bass's career in 1878 in Round Rock, Texas, just north of the capital city of Austin. Bass Outlaw's salary came from arrests made and warrants served. While El Paso was far from a haven of civility, Bass's income hardly supported his own needs, much less those of his newly discovered entertainment partner, a woman named Mercedes. She worked in Tillie Howard's saloon and palace of pleasure on Utah Street, and much to Bass's chagrin, he was not her only client.

On April 4, 1894, Bass accompanied Ware and Deputy Bufe Cline to the federal court in El Paso. Bass was in a bad mood, feeling that many of the warrants under consideration that day should have been his, rather than credited to Cline. Later that afternoon, still in a sullen and dangerous mood and bolstered by his usual quantity of alcohol, Bass left the courthouse and walked to the saloon, seeking solace in the charms of Mercedes. Finding her already occupied, he began ranting and raving, his foul temper becoming even darker.

Inside the saloon sat Constable John Selman, the man who within seventeen months would put Texas's most notorious gunman, John Wesley Hardin, in his grave. Hardin was reportedly so short-tempered that he once shot and killed a man sleeping in an adjoining hotel room simply because the man's snoring disturbed him.

Selman, knowing Bass's reputation and mean streak, had been dogging Little Wolf's trail. Suddenly, from the room Bass had entered came screaming, yelling, and the sound of breaking furniture. Tillie ran outside blowing her police whistle for help. Bass was close behind, trying to take the whistle from the frightened madam.

Bass had been outside only moments when Selman heard gunshots. Rushing out, he saw Bass standing with a smoking gun aimed at Joe McKidrict, a young Ranger. Before Selman could act another shot belched from Bass's pistol, and the bullet entered McKidrict's forehead. Bass fired again as the Ranger fell dead to the ground, hitting him in the back. Thus was fulfilled John Hughes's prediction that Little Wolf would someday kill a Texas Ranger. As far as is known, no other Ranger has ever been killed by an active or former member of the fabled organization.

The ex-Ranger then turned on Selman. Bass, usually an expert marksman, fired at Selman but missed. The bullet sailed by the constable's eye, burning it with gunpowder. Selman, seeing Bass only as a blurred image, calmly raised his revolver and aimed one shot near his target's heart. Bass fired at Selman again, this time severing a blood vessel in his leg and placing a third bullet above the right knee.

Still spitting vinegar and brimstone, Bass jumped a fence and managed to run a hundred yards or so before he came face to face with Ranger Frank McMahon, who unholstered his pistol and announced, "You're under arrest, Bass." Unrepentant, Bass tried to draw a bead on McMahon with his pistol. But Bass was bleeding profusely, and his legs gave way as weakness overtook him and death moved in. McMahon picked him up and carried him inside the Barnum Show Saloon on the corner of Utah and Overland Streets. Without a hint of compassion, McMahon dumped Bass on a pool table.

After examining Bass, local doctor T. S. Turner determined that there was nothing he could do to save the man, or even to make him comfortable. Some men moved Bass to a room in the back of the saloon, where he lingered between life and death for four hours. He finally died lying in a prostitute's bed.

Selman suffered from the three bullets Bass fired at him. It took a couple of weeks of bed rest for him to regain his strength, but he was able to walk thereafter with a cane. While he was not blinded by the gunpowder, Selman's vision never returned to normal. In 1895 he shot and killed the infamous John Wesley Hardin in a saloon in El Paso. About a year after that, Deputy U. S. Marshal George Scarborough shot and killed Selman, also in an El Paso saloon.

As for Bass Outlaw, a witness to his death said that his last sound was a whimper, the kind a wolf tends to make when he knows his time is finished.

7

Lizzie Johnson Williams

EDUCATOR, TRAIL BOSS, RANCHER, MISER

The Chisholm Trail, one of the better-known cattle drive routes in western history, had a lifeline of just seventeen years. In that short period more than six million cattle and horses beat the dirt under their hooves, traveling the trail. Although many men drove herds up the Chisholm from South Texas to Abilene, Kansas, and other cattle towns, it assumed the name of one of the most colorful, influential, successful, and industrious cattlemen ever to mount a horse in Texas. Jesse Chisholm was part Scot, part Cherokee, and left behind a legend that almost seems fictional in its setting.

The cattle drives gave birth to an American ideal still with us today—the mythical yet very real cowboy. Although cattle ceased to be driven up the Chisholm (and other pathways) in the late 1880s, the cowboy continues to roam television, motion pictures, and written media.

History and cowboy tales may revolve around the *men* that made the long, tedious, dangerous drives north, but some very brave women took on the same chore and faced the same hardships. The trails knew no favorites; they treated everyone as equals. Elizabeth "Lizzie" Ellen Johnson was one of the early women, if not the first, to participate in a cattle drive along the Chisholm. It was probably sometime between 1879 and 1884, when the trail drives ended due to the coming of the railroad, that Lizzie climbed aboard her buggy, goosed the horse forward, and ate dust for hundreds of miles as she bossed the crew and herd—cattle bearing her brand—north to market. She probably made less than half a dozen trips on the Chisholm Trail. Even one trip was demanding and turned some men off from making a second journey.

Lizzie, nicknamed "the Cattle Queen of Texas," was not simply an onlooker during the drives. She kept close tabs on the two miles of cattle spread out along the trail. She recorded the hours each of her hands worked and was up each morning before the cattle were ready to move. Because few women made these difficult trips, Lizzie was treated extra special by the cowhands, from the food prepared for her to the guarantees of her safety at night in snake-infested country. Her husband, Hezekiah, accompanied her on the drives, so he received residual benefits from those afforded his wife. At the end of each drive, Lizzie tallied up expenses and recorded profit.

Lizzie was an exceptional individual. She was intelligent, alert to opportunities, and ambitious, and she held little regard for the social mores of the day that relegated women to household chores or the front of school classrooms.

Lizzie was born on May 9, 1840, in Cole County, Missouri, in the center of the state, southwest of the capital, Jefferson City. She was the second of seven children of Thomas Jefferson and Catharine (Hyde) Johnson; her father was a teacher in the public school system, and one of her cousins was Confederate hero General Albert Sidney Johnston. Four years after their daughter's birth, the family moved to Texas and set up house in Huntsville.

Like others before them who had arrived in the land of promise, the Johnsons took a while to settle down. Moving still closer to

Austin, the family lived for a time in Webberville, near the Travis-Bastrop county line. A pious man, Thomas taught school there but was turned off the location because of its proximity to Hell's Half Acre (the red-light district) and a racetrack. There were several Hell's Half Acres in the Old West. They were usually restricted by the gentry to one end of town, and were the sites for rough and rowdy saloons, prostitution, and gunfights. They were normally allowed to operate because the gentlefolk of the town wanted such goings-on to be away from the calmer section of the community. There are reports that Thomas was offered land in Austin (where the University of Texas now sits) to establish a school. He turned down the offer because, according to authors Ann Fears Crawford and Crystal Sasse Ragsdale, he "preferred the unsettled, open spaces far from the temptations of saloons he found in town." The family finally put down roots in Bear Creek, in northeast Hays County close to the Travis County line.

It appears that Thomas was an excellent teacher, versed especially in the fields of mathematics and Latin. With his wife, Catharine, he established the Johnson Institute in Hays County in 1852, with a curriculum stretching from first grade through what today would be recognized as a Bachelor of Arts degree. The school was originally supposed to be for boys only, but so many girls submitted applications that the Johnsons soon made it coed.

Catharine was a woman of many hats: supervisor of household staff; dorm mother; piano teacher; and local doctor when needed. Johnson Institute was the proud possessor of the first piano in Hays County, which Catharine used to teach music in her classroom. Bible studies, although not mandatory, were held on Sunday, and Lizzie read the Bible daily. (In a rather conflicting happenstance, she detested alcohol as an "evil influence" yet later married and was happy with a man who bent the elbow regularly.)

Wedding photograph of Hezekiah G. Williams and Lizzie Johnson,
June 8, 1879

All the Johnson children attended the institute. Lizzie and her brother John later enrolled in private schools in Washington County; John graduated from Soule University and Lizzie, in 1859, from Chappell Hill Female College.

Lizzie followed in her father's footsteps, pursuing a career in education. Her first teaching assignment was in the Johnson Institute. Things changed following the Civil War. Thomas died, and another of Lizzie's brothers, Ben, assumed management of the institute. Annie and Emma, two of Lizzie's sisters, married and moved away.

Lizzie did not garner the same reputation in the classroom that her father had earned. According to Crawford and Ragsdale, she was accused of "being a harsh, unrelenting teacher, and in one instance brought the wrath of the community down on her for her severe punishment of a German boy." Apparently dissatisfied with the restrictions of the institute classroom, Lizzie left in 1863. She taught in nearby Lockhart from 1865 to 1868 and then moved on to Pleasant Hill, where she taught for a year in the Masonic Hall, which still stands today. Her next teaching assignment was in Manor, at the Parsons House, and lasted three years. Lizzie returned to the Johnson Institute in 1871 for a year before moving on to Oak Grove Academy.

Ben closed the institute in 1873, while Lizzie was teaching in Austin.

It was Lizzie's tenure in Lockhart, a gathering spot for ranchers, that ultimately changed the course of her life. Some cattlemen there prevailed upon her to keep books for them. Besides this being one of the subjects Lizzie taught, bookkeeping was a chore most cattlemen dreaded. Lizzie agreed to take on the duty, and thus was set in motion a change that would result in the accumulation of a sizeable personal fortune for the enterprising schoolteacher.

While taking care of the books for the ranchers, Lizzie learned the cattle business. Although she was still teaching in Austin around 1880, that endeavor was set aside. The shrewd bookkeeper saw opportunities that far outweighed any offered in the classroom. Her accounting job brought about meetings with cattlemen like George W. Littlefield, and ranchers such as Charles W. Whitis and William H. Day that further enhanced Lizzie's knowledge of the cattle industry.

(Day, one of the most active cattlemen of the era, was born in Tennessee but had settled in Hays County. He started driving herds north in 1860, the year his father drowned in an accident on the trail. Day continued trail drives, going to Louisiana, St. Louis, and Abilene. He joined up with Jesse Driskill, his brother-in-law, on one drive. Driskill built the hotel in Austin that bears his name and serves as a city landmark. Day died in June 1881 during a trail drive when he was caught in a stampede. Although he left his wife, Mabel Doss Day, near bankruptcy, through ingenuity and perseverance she became another Texas cattle queen.)

Lizzie put her money into cattle stocks, and the investments proved profitable. One reported investment of $2,500, in the Evans, Snider, Bewell Cattle Company of Chicago earned a 300 percent return over three years; she sold the stock for $20,000. She also wrote articles for *Frank Leslie's Illustrated Weekly* and poured earnings from her literary efforts into more stock. Lizzie established a firm financial footing through her investments and expanded into ownership of cattle and land. Moving full time into cattle, she registered a brand (the letters CY) in her name on June 1, 1871. On June 3 she paid Whitis $3,000 in gold for ten acres of land in Austin.

On June 8, 1879, Lizzie married Hezekiah G. Williams, sometimes described as a minister and aspiring developer. Before the ceremony the couple signed a prenuptial agreement stipulating that what was Lizzie's would stay Lizzie's—her property, her money, etc.—and that her financial affairs would be kept separate from her husband's. Hezekiah recognized his wife's acumen in finance and acceded control of most business affairs to her. In fact, Hezekiah often needed to borrow money from his wife. Lizzie considered the transaction a legal contract and made her husband repay all that he borrowed. It is unknown if she charged interest on these loans.

During the early part of their marriage, Lizzie continued to teach school. The couple owned a two-story house on Second Street in Austin. Lizzie used the downstairs for her private school; upstairs served as their personal living quarters.

Hezekiah's vision of becoming a colonizer met with some success. In 1896 the couple bought a ranch located on beautiful rolling hills and situated between the Hays County communities of Kyle and Driftwood. When the county courthouse in San Marcos burned down in 1908, Lizzie and Hezekiah saw the possibility of creating a commercial center on their land. Gathering petitions from like thinkers, they set out to build Hays City, which they hoped would become the new county seat. They laid out plots for a courthouse, churches, a school, and a jail. They even started a newspaper, *The Hays County Enterprise*. From these plans did emerge the construction of a hotel, livery stable, lumberyard, and church.

With plans in hand, the construction of some buildings completed, the backing of many of their neighbors, and the benefits of the area's mineral springs, Lizzie and Hezekiah petitioned the Commissioners Court to call an election to choose a county seat. Hays County was formed in 1848; San Marcos was designated county seat at the same time. Residents, local and regional political and money powers were too strongly entrenched to let an ambitious upstart move in. Consequently, the Williams plan failed, as did Hays City. After their dream fell through, Lizzie and Hezekiah razed all the buildings save the hotel, which later met its fate.

Two streets were laid out in the project: Johnson and Williams. While the development might be a thing of the past, the two streets are still there today.

Lizzie was careful with the family's money, and in some circles people looked on her as a tightwad. However, she did have her extravagances: clothes and diamonds. Running successful cattle and investment operations afforded Lizzie and her husband the luxury of travel and shopping, two pursuits that delighted Lizzie. One of their favorite stops was St. Louis, where other cattlemen of means congregated with their wives. Here Lizzie indulged her appetite for the latest fashions displayed on the pages of *Frank Leslie's Illustrated Weekly*: velvets, brocades, and laces. She splurged on shoes of the day and hats for different occasions and seasons.

In New York she "giddily spent $10,000 on jewelry alone," according to Crawford and Ragsdale. "Choosing a pair of two-carat diamond earrings, she supplemented them with a tiara containing a center diamond of three carats surrounded by nine half-carat stones and a sunburst pin with eighty-four diamonds in a gold setting."

Lizzie did not stuff her jewelry away like a pack rat in some safe or cache; she wore it openly and often. Sometimes it appeared that she flaunted her affluence to draw attention, and draw attention she did. In 1916, at the age of seventy-six, she was invited to her nephew's wedding. She rode up to the church in a wagon pulled by two white horses. Lizzie sashayed into the church wearing a beautiful dress and decked out with rings, a pin covered with diamonds, and an encrusted tiara mounted firmly in her hair.

In their years of health and wealth, Lizzie and her husband spent some time traveling abroad. A controversial tale revolves around the alleged kidnapping of Hezekiah in Havana. The "kidnappers" demanded a ransom of $50,000, which Lizzie paid without blinking an eye. There is some speculation that Hezekiah arranged his own kidnapping for the money, since his wife held a tight grip on the purse strings.

When Hezekiah's health took a sudden turn for the worse (he had been a heavy drinker for most of his life), Lizzie took him to Hot Springs, Arkansas, where they hoped the medicinal waters would affect a cure. Unfortunately, the springs seemed to make him worse. Thinking El Paso's warm climate might offer hope, Lizzie and her husband traveled to the far southwestern tip of Texas. The trip was a futile effort; Hezekiah died there in 1914. Lizzie brought his body back to Austin and had him buried there, at a cost of $600. When presented the bill, she paid it in full and then scribbled across the face of the bill, "I loved this old buzzard this much."

The passing of Hezekiah threw Lizzie into a state of melancholy and bitterness. Friends and acquaintances described her as becoming a recluse and eccentric. She had never been close to her relatives, even her brothers and sisters, so familial contact was practically nonexistent. While Lizzie had always been frugal with money, except for her personal desires, she became a miser and appeared to be living in a state of near poverty.

Hezekiah had signed over his estate to Lizzie in July 1896 (although the transfer did not become official until 1913). It included the Brueggerhoff Building, situated on the corner of Tenth Street and Congress Avenue in Austin. Always wise in the ways of money, Lizzie lived on the second floor of the building and rented out the remaining rooms. The older she got, the more money she acquired and the more miserly she became. As author Emily Jones Shelton notes, "She heated the Brueggerhoff Building with wood stoves. All the wood was locked in one room and issued to her tenants stick by stick."

The story is told of Lizzie making daily trips to the Maverick Cafe on Congress Avenue, where she indulged in a bowl of vegetable soup with crackers for 10 cents. When the weather turned cold and fresh vegetables were hard to come by, the cafe upped its price for the soup. Lizzie, beguiling and seemingly destitute, convinced the owner to continue charging her only 10 cents a bowl.

Another tale indicates that Lizzie began to pay less and less attention to her personal appearance, especially her dress. While at the post office picking up her mail, she was dressed so shabbily that strangers offered her money. Unbeknownst to them, she probably could have bought and sold most of them many times over.

Even late in life, when she was virtually cut off from the public and family, Lizzie continued to conduct her business affairs—from borrowing money to indulging in stocks to paying off debts. Once, as matters go, Lizzie walked into a bank where she owed several thousand dollars. After asking for her note, she proceeded to pull from her purse a red bandana. Laying the kerchief on the manager's desk, she counted out to the penny the amount of the note.

Time would not spare even the Cattle Queen of Texas. When it became apparent that she could no longer take care of herself, Lizzie moved in with her niece, Willie Greer Shelton, and Shelton's husband, John. Lizzie was comfortable in her new surroundings, and the family treated her well. But she had had a full life, and the waning days of that life played heavily on her mind. She was not in *her* house. Her husband had passed on. The ranch no longer offered her solace. Everything was passing by. Lizzie realized that fact but, like most people in a similar situation, hated to admit it or accept it.

When she passed away on October 9, 1924, officials were surprised to discover that the value of Lizzie's estate exceeded a quarter million dollars. They also discovered that although she feigned miserliness, her apartment contained a well-stocked closet of fine clothing and a trove of diamond jewelry. In addition, her personal papers revealed that she had extensive holdings in real estate. She owned land in Culbertson, Hays, Jeff Davis, Llano, Travis, and Trinity Counties.

Lizzie, having no children, left no will. Acquaintances were not surprised at this lapse, claiming, "She didn't feel she needed one. She planned to take it all with her."

The ranch, covering some six hundred acres, went through a succession of owners and renters. In 1942 Walter Prescott Webb, renowned historian and history professor at the University of Texas, bought the property. He and his wife, Jane, restored the old buildings and constructed new ones. They rechristened the site Friday Mountain, taking the moniker from a small nearby rise. The hill acquired its name because that was the day of the week surveyors came into the area. The Webbs established the ranch as a writer's retreat.

Webb and a friend, Rodney J. Kidd, met in November 1946 and drew up plans for a boys' summer camp to be located on the grounds. The Friday Mountain Camp for Boys opened in 1947 and operated for almost four decades. Kidd later purchased the site from Webb and sold off much of the land. Today, the old Williams Ranch is home to one of the largest Hindu temples in North America.

From her burial plot in Austin's Oakwood Cemetery, Lizzie Johnson Williams is no doubt surprised by these transformations. But after a full and rewarding life, the early Texas female entrepreneur can finally rest easy.

8

Wild Man of the Navidad

"THE THING THAT COMES"

The Navidad River starts its southeasterly, seventy-four-mile journey near the town of Schulenburg in Fayette County. The waterway, named by the Spanish for the Nativity of Christ, ends its travels where it joins the Lavaca River below Lake Texana in Jackson County. The river cuts across today's Highway 90A between Hallettsville, the Lavaca County seat, and the small community of Sublime to the east. The stream is short, virtually nonnavigable, and limited in recreational benefit. But there was a time when the Navidad had a mystery all its own.

In the mid-1830s a particular section of Navidad bottomlands in Jackson County was home to an unidentifiable creature that stirred up rumors and speculation for miles around. A yeti? The Abominable Snowman? Whatever he—or it—was, the mysterious figure managed to avoid detection and capture for more than sixteen years. The first indication that a ghost or some other illusive figure traversed the bottomlands occurred in 1834. Settlers began noticing that sometime during the night, someone was breaking into homes and stealing food. At that time the area was sparsely populated, and it was possible for such sneaking about to take place. There were, however, some puzzling aspects to these robberies.

The intruder was able to pass watchdogs that continued sleeping and did little watching. Once inside, whoever was stealing food took only half of what was in the larder, leaving the other half completely untouched. The oddest quirk of the episodes was that the intruder completely ignored items of value, such as money and jewelry, but often took tools and kitchen utensils. The implements were returned sometime later, having been shined and sharpened and generally made as good as new. The invader did not limit his purloining to food from inside the homes. He often ran off with vegetables from gardens and fruit that the occupants had picked. One of his boldest tricks took place during slaughtering season. He sneaked onto farmers' sites and replaced fatted hogs with skinny ones.

The thief also took clothing hung on lines to dry. This was a real puzzler because when the individual was finally spotted, he was wearing only a loincloth around his hips. No trace of the stolen clothes was ever found, and, as far as anyone can tell, he never wore them.

Fact or fiction? Who, or what, was this unexplainable creature? Recorded incidents prove that the so-called Wild Man of the Navidad was definitely not fiction. In 1850 hunters in the area organized a posse to seek out the man of mystery. With the aid of numerous search dogs, the posse was finally able to track him down. They forced their quarry to climb a tree in an attempt to avoid capture. The men did not intend to harm him, so they called for him to come down. The Wild Man either did not understand English or feared what would become of him if captured. He neither responded nor alit from his haven in the tree. Eventually, a member of the gang climbed the tree and brought him down.

The hunters were not surprised at the appearance of their dark-skinned captive. He looked pretty much as witnesses had described him over the years. Since people could not understand the language the man spoke, or he theirs, the locals put him in jail—mainly for his own protection. Capture of the Wild Man of the Navidad, who might as well have been a mute as far as communication went, attracted attention and publicity far and wide.

The mystery of the Wild Man eventually saw daylight, although the explanations we have today vary by source. Some say that a trader (or sailor) who coincidentally spoke the detainee's dialect happened to be traveling through the area and heard the story of the prisoner. After talking with the man, the trader learned that he was the son of an African chieftain and had been sold to a slave trader for a knife and tobacco. Once on Texas soil, the man and a companion had escaped and traveled north until they reached the Navidad bottomlands. They were so successful at entering homes in the middle of the night undetected because, in Africa, they knew that dogs slept more soundly at certain times. The captive relayed that his companion had died, probably from exposure, a few years after they settled in the bottomlands.

Another version of the Texas Yeti is that he was a slave owned by plantation lord Ben Fort Smith, whose property was located in Grimes County. It was from this site that the Wild Man fled. And it was rumored that he took a black or Indian woman with him, along with a second male escapee.

J. Frank Dobie, renowned historian, professor, and writer, presents yet another account of the Wild Man. In his book *Tales of Old-Time Texas,* Dobie writes that planters whose land was watered by the Brazos River, south of the city of Richmond, bought a number of slaves to work their plantations; this was excellent soil for cotton. Several slaves escaped into the thick Piney Woods, with some traveling on to Mexico and others joining up with or becoming slaves to the Cronk Indians. According to Dobie, at least one escapee made it to the Navidad

Some Navidad River bottomland where the "Wildman" roamed at one time

bottomlands. He was "a giant in strength and was almost as fleet on foot as an ordinary cow pony."

The Wild Man possessed a "guttural" voice, and although he caused no harm and no one wanted to kill him, he did provoke a scare in the womenfolk and children. Mothers put the fear of the devil in their misbehaving children "by threatening them with the 'Wild Black Man.'" Other slaves in the river area of Lavaca and Jackson Counties called the forest creature "the thing that comes," comparing his appearance and actions to a ghost.

Had the Wild Man's capture occurred fifteen years or so later, he probably would have been released from jail and taught the English language, or perhaps exploited as a freak by some circus entrepreneur. As it was the 1850s and the man was captured in Texas, a slave state, he enjoyed only momentary freedom—ironically while jailed. He was later sold to P. T. Bickford of Refugio County for $207, the purchase made at the slave block in Victoria on August 1, 1851. Bickford did not enjoy any services for his money. Before the day was out, the slave escaped.

As was par for the day, Bickford gave him a new name, the anglicized Jimbo, before he even bought him off the slave block. There is no record of who actually put the Wild Man on the slave block or whose property he became upon capture. Zebrian Lewis of Victoria County subsequently became master to Jimbo and held him in servitude until he received his freedom in 1865.

The story goes that Jimbo received his freedom after the Civil War. Supposedly, he hooked up with the Carlos Ranch in southwestern Victoria County. The year of his death is listed as 1884. Jimbo never learned English, and his only mode of oral communication was broken Spanish, which listeners claimed was virtually indecipherable.

Why did Jimbo not receive more publicity during his lifetime? After all, thirty-four years passed from the time of his capture until his death. That the Wild Man was able to live free, avoid capture, and yet not harm anyone—or personally sustain harm—is a phenomenon itself.

How Jimbo faded from public view after his capture and remained isolated for more than three decades is as big a mystery as his existence and exploits. It is highly unlikely that the full mystery of the Wild Man of the Navidad will ever be explained.

Add a gender twist, and the story gets even more interesting. Dobie suggests that it was a woman—not a man—who undertook the mysterious capers. He bases this assertion on the belief that the man hunters captured in 1850 was too old and too fragile to have accomplished many of the feats credited to him.

Dobie writes about an incident that took place in the Navidad area in 1846. Some men were combing the land for the Wild Man when they spotted a figure running across an open expanse toward a wooded glen. They attempted to capture the individual, but even though they were on horseback, it evaded their chase as well as the lassoes thrown to entangle it. The rider who came closest to capturing the figure described it as having "long, flowing hair that trailed down almost to its feet" and said that it "wore no clothes . . . her body seemed covered entirely by short, brown hair."

Both descriptions are explainable. The Wild Man had no contact with barbers during his many years in the forest—ergo, no haircut. As for the body appearance, the man was black and had been running free for years. His skin could have taken on different appearances depending on the flora and fauna with which he had come in contact.

Nevertheless, if there was a Wild Woman instead of a Wild Man, she might have found a kindred soul in a local resident. Some people in the area at the time wanted to connect romantically the distaff side of the forest fugitive with Moses Evans, a Kentuckian who fought in Texas's struggle for independence. He was often described as a wild man, with "flowing red hair and a beard to match." Evans eschewed things civilized, at least to a limit. He lived in and off the woods but would come into the community and dance with the ladies. His lack of bathing and use of animal skins that were not fully cured for clothing often repelled not only people with whom he came in contact, but his own nasal sense as well.

The Wild Man of the Woods, as Evans was tagged, and the Wild Woman of the Navidad were not fated to meet. This did not prevent matchmakers from attempting to spark a romance between the two by composing numerous poems and love letters that were published in local and state newspapers. These epistles of love had to be read to Evans since he could neither read nor write. He reveled in the attention anyway.

Despite being illiterate, Evans served as a surveyor and accumulated much land in East Texas. He died on October 6, 1853, at the young age of forty-three and was interred in Washington County Cemetery.

As for the Wild Man (or Woman) of the Navidad, can we believe that people originally thought it was an otherworldly creature? Certainly. After all, today in East Texas there is an organization called the Texas Bigfoot Research Center, whose members are "dedicated to finding the Lone Star State's Sasquatch." Even in this enlightened—and skeptical—age, there will always be believers in the supernatural.

9

Adah Isaacs Menken

WAS SHE REALLY NAKED?

People who are familiar with the *New York Times* crossword puzzles advise that if you attempt to solve them, you should do so in pencil, never in ink. The pencil advice also applies to anyone writing about actress and poet Adah Isaacs Menken.

No one, at least in so-called modern times, has packed so much living in a life that spanned just thirty-three years. Yet, though she was once renowned on two continents, Adah remains an enigma wrapped in a mystery that, unlike the crossword puzzle, defies solution. In her brief lifetime Adah married four times (that we know of), gave her love to many, was the highest-paid female performer of her day, and became an intimate friend of many literary talents of the time—yet she was virtually ignored at her own funeral.

Adah was her own, and best, publicity agent, always changing the details of her accomplishments and personal background (including her ethnicity and lineage) to fit the environment of the moment. Most of all, she carried her stage persona into real life, so much so that it was difficult, if not impossible, to separate the two.

Her constant self-rebirth led many historians and biographers to draw their own conclusions and make up what they could not prove.

As Gregory Eiselein notes, "Most of the biographical and critical work on . . . Adah Isaacs Menken is dreadful. From mass-market biographies published in her lifetime to recent reference books, the recording and interpreting of Menken's life has been unreliable, misleading, poorly documented, and distorted by an array of biases." And yet much of the blame has to be placed on the subject herself. Adah lived in a self-constructed kaleidoscope that she turned to suit her purposes.

Early thinking was that Adah was born in Chartrain (now Milneburg), Louisiana, a suburb of New Orleans. Supposedly, her family was of Jewish origin, although this seems a dubious claim at best. Her father was a free black man, and her mother was a Creole. This cultural mix might account for Adah throwing her past to the wind and letting various and questionable details float as they might. Neither ethnic group, black nor Creole, points to a Jewish influence. Adah did become a Jewish convert, however, and remained so until the day she died.

At least one biographer lists Adah's birth surname as McCord and her date of birth as June 15, 1835; this is the year Adah always confirmed. She was the eldest of three children from the union of Richard and Catherine McCord. Adah claimed, at varying times, to have been born Adelaide McCord, Ada Bertha Théodore, Rachel Adah Isaacs, Dolores Adios Fuertos, and Marie Rachel Adelaide de Vere Spenser. The film of puzzlement did not stop with her own name. She also created different monikers for her parents, siblings, and even for a stepfather she referred to as either Dr. J. C. Campbell or simply Israels.

In Adah's own tellings, her places of birth ranged from Nacogdoches, Texas, to the Louisiana locales of Chartrain, Milneburg, and New Orleans; to Memphis, Tennessee; and to an unnamed site in Spain. As for her ethnicity, she pretty much covered all groups, including Creole, French, Jewish, African American, Scotch-Irish, and Spanish.

She played the ethnic card she thought would benefit her most at any particular time.

There have been many attempts to discern the truth behind this enigmatic woman of talent, who knew exactly what she wanted, knew how to get it, and was willing to travel any road to achieve her end. And she did accomplish most of what she set out to do. Adah was certainly a female with a Machiavellian attitude.

Her talent for entertaining came early. She exhibited a flair for singing and dancing and by her own admission was once a sculptor's model and a circus performer who rode horses (a skill that would bring her fame and fortune later). Adah danced in the New Orleans French Opera House, where she was a member of the ballet line. Shortly thereafter, she appeared with a ballet troupe in Havana, Cuba, where, even as a child, she attracted attention and by some reports was crowned "Queen of the Plaza." As far as can be discerned, Havana was Adah's swan song as a ballerina. Upon her return to America, she turned her talents to stage roles.

Her Texas connection may have begun in the early 1850s, when she reportedly was known as Adelaide McCord and lived in a log cabin in Nacogdoches with her parents. Some sources suggest that she was enrolled in Nacogdoches University, although no records exist to prove this claim. It was in the East Texas town that Adah supposedly met and captivated Thomas Peck Ochiltree, then a Texas Ranger and later a Civil War officer and Texas politician.

After Tom's death in 1902, an article, apparently gleaned from his notes, appeared in the *St Louis Globe-Democrat*. The article left no doubt about the Texian's infatuation with the dark-eyed Adah, who was described as "strikingly pretty . . . schoolboys vied with one another to carry her books, while old men were charmed into stuffing her pockets with gold coins. Adah's figure blossomed early

Courtesy of The Harvard Theatre Collection, Houghton Library

Adah Isaacs Menken as Don Leon in Children of the Sun

and by her late teens she was already earning the reputation of a flirt."

Tom and Adah may have reunited in Paris in 1867, when some claim she was married to the King of Württemberg, but that flamboyant story is unverified. One thing's for certain: Adah was in Texas in October 1855. She did readings of Shakespeare in Austin and the small East Texas town of Washington. Rumor has it that while hunting buffalo that same year near Port Lavaca, she was captured by Indians. The Texas Rangers, under the command of Frederick Harney, rescued her. Harney apparently adopted her, but when Adah fell in love with her benefactor, he sent her away. Sam Houston supposedly also adopted the young lady. Dissatisfied with her surroundings, Adah left the confining household of the Houston abode and traveled to Mexico with a ballet troupe. These escapades may have been complete fabrications on her part, but they certainly fit into the adventurous persona she cultivated.

Adah met her first husband, Alexander Isaac Menken, while both were performing at Neitsch's Theater in Galveston. They fell in love yet did not get married in the port city. Instead, the pair ran off to Livingston, where they joined hands on April 3, 1856, she under the name Ada B. Théodore. Why the couple chose Livingston as a wedding site has never been explained. It is some one hundred miles north of Galveston, and in the mid-1800s the journey would have taken three to four days under the best of conditions.

Her union with Alexander was the first of several marriages for the flamboyant chanteuse (some sources list as many as seven, but verification exists for only four). Menken, who was from a prominent Ohio Jewish family, saw in Adah a beautiful, charming, intelligent woman—the ideal mother of his future children. Whereas family was uppermost in his priorities, motherhood was the lowest rung on Adah's ladder of ambition. She was a free spirit with only one interest: the stage.

The newlyweds did not return to Galveston. Instead, they went to New Orleans, where they reportedly resided with Adah's younger sister and widowed mother. The year after their wedding, Adah and Alexander moved to Cincinnati, at her insistence. Perhaps she needed a rest from appearances in small theaters in Nashville, New Orleans, and Shreveport. It was in Cincinnati that she converted to Judaism and immersed herself in the practice, even learning to read Hebrew. She took on Jewish causes and during her short lifespan carried the Star of David proudly. According to author Seymour Brody, "she never performed on Yom Kippur and she slept with a Hebrew Bible under her pillow." He notes that Adah also railed against the exclusion of Jews from the British House of Commons.

Although not wealthy, Alexander was a man of some means. As long as he was the breadwinner in the family, their marriage flowed smoothly. In 1857 things changed. Alexander's investments plunged as banks called in loans involving overextended western railroads. By the time dust from the financial fiasco settled, he was virtually penniless. All of a sudden Adah was the couple's sole support. Such a situation can breed hard feelings in the best of times, but in an era when the husband was looked on as the main support of his family, failure to maintain his status became degrading.

The events of the day did little to dampen Adah's enthusiasm. To the contrary, she was more than willing to earn the family's income and immediately decided to once again trip the light fantastic and resume her theatrical career. In 1857 in Shreveport, Louisiana, she had the role of Pauline in *The Lady of Lyons, or Love and Pride*. A short time later, she was on the stage in New Orleans as Bianca in *Fazio*. Adah also began writing poetry, with some of her work appearing in the *Cincinnati Israelite* and the *New York Sunday Mercury*. Her efforts with rhyme appeared in print from 1857 to 1861, although Adah asserted that in 1856, under the nom de plume Indigena, she had published a book of poems titled *Memories*.

In February 1858 Adah jumped at the chance to play Lady Macbeth. Her performance was completely against type and a near disaster; it was the last time she attempted Shakespeare. Later that year, she signed on for a role in *Sixteen-String Jack* in Dayton, Ohio. In the audience during her performance was a raucous group of some seventy-five members of the Dakota Light Guard, a voluntary militia group. The men whistled and applauded whenever Adah appeared on stage. Following the performance, delegates from the group went to the star's dressing room and, after gushing over her, invited Adah to be the guest of honor at dinner at a local hotel. Adah graciously accepted the kind offer. During the gala affair she was "commissioned" an honorary captain of the Light Guard. After the festivities Adah reportedly went to her room, where she remained—alone—for the rest of the night.

Simply by force of her personality and lack of inhibitions, Adah garnered a negative reputation. By the time she returned to Cincinnati, all types of scandalous stories had traveled the sixty miles from Dayton and found residence in Alexander's troubled mind. When he confronted his wife with the rumors, she explained what had really happened. He said he believed her, which quickly proved untrue. Alexander accused his wife of tarnishing the family name with her exploits and careless ways. He demanded that she give up her theatrical aspirations and become a proper wife.

They argued and Alexander stormed out of the house, threatening to never return home. After a few months of separation, Adah gave in and begged him to return. She promised to do nothing in the future that might degrade the Menken name. And, for a while, she stayed true to her vow. But the lure of footlights and applause was too strong. She had to perform. When she approached Alexander about returning to the stage, he adamantly opposed the idea, although she pledged to hold herself in refined decorum.

Adah had her way, however, when she brought up their financial situation, which was at low ebb. Alexander, as much as he resented it, knew that his wife was the only one that could earn a living. She was doing what she wanted—performing in public; he was standing in the wings, a virtual nonentity.

The union between Adah and Alexander might have continued along its boring way had not Adah met Adonis. At Christmastime in 1858 she was at the New National Theater in Cincinnati in a production of Sir Walter Scott's *Ivanhoe*. As a side attraction to the night's entertainment, self-proclaimed American heavyweight titleholder John Carmel Heenan appeared in a one-round exhibition. Adah had never heard of John. The lure of anyone involved in fisticuffs for a living held no appeal to the thespian.

Fate has a way of unexpectedly exerting its influence. Adah was preparing to depart for home after her performance when the theater manager brought John to her dressing room for an introduction. Despite her indifference toward anyone in the fighting field, she was smitten like a young schoolgirl when she set eyes on the tall, handsome, godlike man towering over her. John, in turn, was awestruck by the beautiful woman and could not take his eyes off her.

Their meeting was over in a matter of minutes. The scene caused Adah to begin comparing—unfairly, of course—Alexander to this near-perfect specimen of manhood. The rickety Menken marriage underwent further cracks as Adah started finding more faults in her husband. She often thought of Alexander as a gofer, an errand boy, but this had never bothered her before. After standing next to Heenan, her mate looked paler and paler.

Adah could not live up to her promise to ride the trail of societal niceness and decorum. She was bohemian to the core and neither denied it nor tried to cover it. Her shenanigans were too much for the Menken family. Alexander's affluent parents did not consider Adah worthy of their son and deplored the attention and fawning she received as a stage actress. Alexander went his way and Adah hers, with their divorce supposedly secured by a rabbinical diploma. She carried the Menken name as her own until she died but for some reason added an s to Alexander's middle name. Adah never saw him again.

Free from what she considered marital entanglement, Adah threw herself into the theater. Her beauty and grace, voluptuous figure, and derring-do performances brought her much desired attention. "Stage-door Johnnies" filled the theater alleyways. If she did not garner enough attention naturally, Adah made sure that she received publicity by placing pictures of herself in every store window in the towns where she appeared. In fact, Adah has been acknowledged as the "first person to become a celebrity through photographs" (see Van-meenen), a fairly new approach at the time.

Adah married Heenan on September 3, 1859. The boxing champion taught her the finer points of fisticuffs, but he soon turned tyrant and started using his wife as a punching bag. In 1860 he traveled to London to train for a fight with British pugilist Tom Sayers. Adah wanted to accompany her husband, but Heenan and his promoter refused to take her. At this time Adah was pregnant and had great trepidation about the child being born without Heenan present. He did not know of Adah's condition and she refused to tell him, not wanting to burden him at the time of a tremendous step in his career.

Heenan and Sayers fought forty-two rounds in April 1860. Heenan's face was covered with blood, rendering him practically blind, and Sayers had a broken arm. Fans stormed the ring and declared the bout a draw. Sportswriters on both sides of the Atlantic naturally claimed the title for their boy. This fight preceded the days of boxing gloves. Two men stood in the ring and pounded away at each other—bare-knuckle style—until one or both of them could no longer stand.

Ever the opportunist, Adah realized the publicity value of her husband's name and began billing herself as Mrs. John Carmel Heenan. The result was overflowing audiences in Boston's National Theater and the Old Bowery Theater in New York. Still in England, Heenan resented the fact that Adah was capitalizing on his name.

He was not the only one who objected. When Alexander Menken learned of Adah's new billing, he went into a rage. He wrote a letter to the *Cincinnati Commercial* denying that he and Adah were ever divorced. Alexander continued his diatribe: "[I]n the State of Texas I had the misfortune to be married by a Justice of the Peace, to the adventuress, since which time I have never been divorced from her.

I . . . have instituted proceedings in the proper courts which will rid me of this incubus and disgrace."

Whereas his words were fraught with sour grapes and venom, Adah's reply, also printed in the *Commercial,* was subdued. She reported no ill will toward Alexander and refused to engage in what she termed "garbage journalism." She did make the point, which Alexander could not deny, that during their union her husband was "nourished by, and subsisted upon, the fruits of my professional labor, until I would no longer furnish supplies for his bacchanalian career." No more was heard from Alexander, other than the final divorce decree.

Heenan learned of the Menken mess and felt he had been betrayed. The boxer denied that he and Adah were ever married. The *New York Sunday Mercury* challenged this last claim and offered to produce the ministering official at the wedding, as well as the witnesses.

Adah once again felt the sting of bad publicity. She was getting no money from Heenan and was continuing to perform despite her pregnancy. Her health began to deteriorate. Months went by without a word from her husband. Distance fuels rumor, and Adah believed that Heenan had taken up with another woman. Adah gave birth to a baby boy in June 1860 and hoped that the child would keep Heenan from turning his back on their union. The baby died soon after birth, however, and Adah knew that her marriage was in shambles.

Heenan returned to New York in August 1860 a hero, with reporters following his every word. He denied being married to Adah and, through his lawyer, claimed that she was no more than a prostitute. She sued Heenan in August 1861 and turned the tables on her badmouthing husband. The grounds for her suit were "non-support, abandonment, and adultery, 'with one Harriet Morgan, in the city of Chicago.'" The divorce was granted in April 1862.

In the meantime Adah had continued her quest for the limelight. In 1859 she went on a short-lived vaudeville tour with Jean Francois Gravelet, who performed under the name Blondin. And she walked onstage again, appearing in *The Soldier's Daughter, The French Spy,* and *Black-Eyed Susan.*

For fun she ventured into nightspots where "decent" women never went. Adah never put on airs about being decent; she was free-spirited and reveled in the attention it brought her. One of New York's most popular establishments at the time was Charley Pfaff's, a beer cellar. There Adah drank and smoked and was treated as an equal by such luminaries as George Arnold, famous for his quotes, and science fiction writer Fitz-James O'Brien. William Thackeray and Walt Whitman, popular in their own rights, often occupied seats at Adah's "roundtable."

Another man whom Adah met changed her life ever after. He was Jimmie Murdock, and he became her business manager. Jimmie surmised that Adah's experience and talent precluded any great stage dramas. But he saw a light in the beautiful woman's eyes and knew just where it should shine.

Broadway was hosting the play *Mazeppa,* based on a poem by George Gordon, Lord Byron. While the play itself was heavy, the climatic ending stirred a rousing feeling in the audience. Mazeppa, the young Tartar prince, rides off—stripped naked and tied to a horse—across papier-mâché mountains. Because the stunt was dangerous, a dummy was usually strapped to the horse. Jimmie thought Adah was perfect for the title role, and she got it in June 1861 in Albany, New York—but she would have none of the dummy taking her place.

For the famous scene Adah wore a skintight outfit that left little to the imagination. In his biographical sketch of Adah, Samuel Dickinson reports that the "audience was shocked—scandalized—horrified—*and*

delighted!" Despite the raves, New Yorkers at the time were not recep-
tive to such a display. Feeling rebuffed but elated by her performances,
Adah decided to move *Mazeppa* to a more acceptable viewing site: San
Francisco. This proved to be one of the more fortuitous steps in Adah's
complicated, captivating life.

Her star had risen; she found her magnum opus in *Mazeppa*.
Adah took the show to San Francisco in August 1863 and became
queen of the City by the Bay. She had sixteen performances there, and
each was a sellout. It was the perfect setting for someone of Adah's
temperament and lack of inhibition. The gold strike fever had ebbed
by this time, but San Francisco was a wild and wooly place, especially
the northeastern section of the city.

Tom Maguire, owner of Maguire's Opera House, welcomed
Adah with open arms. According to Dickinson, Tom's advertisements
promised that "Miss Menken, stripped by her captors, will ride a fiery
steed at furious gallop onto and across the stage and into the distance." The fact that Adah was not actually naked played no part in
Maguire's publicity.

Local newspapers declared that opening night was a rousing success. Diamonds glittered on well-to-do women escorted by splendidly
dressed husbands and escorts. The street in front of the opera house
was congested with carriages. The crowd was not disappointed. Adah
put on a performance long remembered by those in the audience and
extolled by the newspapers covering the show. In Dickinson's words,
as Adah rode across the stage strapped to a California horse, "the
enthusiasm of the audience was a mad frenzy never to be forgotten."

Three years after her appearance in Albany, Adah performed
Mazeppa in London. She took the British by storm and soon became an
associate of Algernon Charles Swinburne, Charles Dickens, and Dante
Gabriel Rossetti. Rumors surfaced that Adah and Swinburne were more

than friends; he supposedly whispered to her, "My darling, a woman with such beautiful legs as yours need not bother about poetry."

Adah returned to New York in 1865 and performed to great acclaim. She toured the United States before going back to Europe the following year. Her stage résumé expanded to include such plays as *Dick Turpin, Three Fast Women,* and *The Child of the Sun.* No matter how her other efforts were received, the call always went back to *Mazeppa* and her "nude" performance.

Adah was married at least two more times. From 1862 to 1865 she carried the name of Robert Henry Newell, a journalist and humorist. Born in New York City on December 13, 1836, Newell was at one time or another literary editor of *New York Sunday Mercury,* a columnist for *New York World,* and editor of *Hearth and Home.* His satirical work, for which he is best known, appeared under the pen name Orpheus C. Kerr, which some historians morphed into "office seeker."

Newell was of a puritanical bent—something that Adah neither was nor ever wanted to be. Her new husband was well aware of his wife's persona. He had known her for a long time and had spoken words of endearment for at least a month before they married. Yet after they wed, Newell said no when Adah wanted to go out and hit the nightspots. Her place was in the home, not out gadding about in smoke-filled cabarets.

When Adah displayed a determination to go anyway, Newell forcibly locked her in a bedroom. Undeterred, she climbed out a window and took off to be with her unorthodox cronies. Newell later begged to be taken back and admitted he had made a terrible mistake. Adah relented, but the marriage, for all practical purposes, was over. Back in New York, she filed for divorce, charging Newell with abandonment. He did not contest the proceedings, and Adah was again granted her freedom.

Adah's next walk down the matrimonial aisle was in 1866, to James Paul Barkley, a broker (or merchant or professional gambler; he has been described variously). She was in London at the time, performing *Mazeppa* at the Astley Theatre. Adoring crowds followed Adah everywhere she went; police escorts had to protect her from the worshipping onrush. During her stay Adah resided in suites at the Westminster Palace Hotel, where she entertained literary notables such as Swinburne and Rossetti. Barkley was a frequent guest. When he sailed to America, she was not far behind. Adah once again appeared onstage in *Mazeppa*, at the Broadway Theater in 1866. She moved on, taking the play to Boston and Washington.

She was in Washington when she discovered that she was pregnant. Adah hurried back to New York, where she and Barkley were married. The union served only to give the baby a legitimate father, an issue of prime importance in those days. The marriage was over three days later. Adah had by then realized that the matrimonial path was not for her—too confining.

Adah's second pregnancy ended as the first had: The baby boy, named Louis Duderant Victor Emmanuel, died shortly after birth. After a brief period of recuperation, Adah packed up and moved to Paris. She might have adopted her lifestyle from Paris native (and godmother to doomed baby Louis) Amandine Lucile Aurore Dupin, or George Sand. The writer was infamous for her affairs with composer Frédéric Chopin and poet Alfred de Musset. Defying social convention was a part of Sand's daily life.

Adah's feelings on motherhood are unknown. She did have a peculiar slant on marriage, though. Authors David Wallechinsky and Irving Wallace excerpt one of her letters to a friend: "I believe all good men should be married. Yet I don't believe in women being married. Somehow they all sink into nonentities after this epoch in their existence. That is the fault of the female education. They are taught from their cradles to look upon marriage as the one event of their lives. That accomplished, nothing remains."

Adah conquered Paris as she had conquered every other location. Rock stars of today would recognize the wildness that surrounded her every waking moment. Police escorts and bodyguards were routine parts of her entourage. Menken memorabilia—ranging from hats, coats, and shaving mugs to cravats and collars—were vended on every street. Both her beauty and her acting received accolades loudly and often. Had she been so inclined, Adah might have become the consort of Emperor Napoleon III, who attended her performances.

Her audience expanded. She toured Paris and Vienna to wide enthusiasm. Adah gave her final performance at Sadler's Wells Theatre in London. She collapsed during rehearsal for *Les Pirates de la Savane* on May 30, 1868, and was moved to her hotel. She complained of pains in her side, but a final diagnosis was never released. The pain was probably from an accident she incurred on an earlier excursion to London. Some conjecture has it that she died from tuberculosis or possibly cancer. Her only companion as she crossed over the threshold of life at age thirty-three was a maid.

The admiration and worship accorded Adah in life did not follow to her Paris gravesite. She was interred in Père Lachaise but later reburied in the Jewish section of Montparnasse. Whereas hundreds followed her whenever she was in the public eye, only a dozen or so mourners were in the funeral cortege, followed by the horse that had served her so well in *Mazeppa*. Notable by their absence were her former husbands and lovers.

Infelicia, a collection of poems that Adah had dedicated to Charles Dickens, was published in London ten days after her death.

Adah lived life lavishly and to the fullest. At one time she was the highest-paid female performer in America, earning as much as $500 a night. Despite all the money she had made in some eleven years on the stage, she was virtually a pauper when she died. That is only further proof that Adah Isaacs Menken lived her life as she rode her horse: recklessly and fully. She would have had it no other way.

10

Three-Legged Willie

JUSTICE AND INDEPENDENCE ABOVE ALL

If the trite adage "When given a lemon, make lemonade" ever applied to an individual, that person would be legendary Texas judge and lawmaker Robert McAlpin Williamson. The year was about 1821, and Williamson was fifteen, the age when boys suddenly had to grow up; they were either behind a plow, working at a trade, or in school. For Williamson the year would be one of fate. His life was altered—against his will.

Williamson was afflicted with an ailment known as "white swelling," a chronic condition that caused his right leg to bend in a permanent position at the knee and stay parallel to the ground. As the story goes, he designed a peg leg that went from his knee to the floor. The apparatus earned him the nickname "Three-Legged Willie." He also designed specially tailored clothes to fit over all three "legs." There is speculation that he had previously suffered from a case of infantile paralysis.

No one knows why Williamson did not have the lower part of his leg amputated and replaced by an artificial limb. Although medical science back then was primitive compared to today, such operations were not uncommon. Mexican general Antonio López de Santa Anna lost a leg fighting the French in 1838 and functioned quite well for several years thereafter.

Williamson had to stay out of school for two years while he recuperated. But those years were not wasted. He spent the time reading and learning, and at age nineteen he joined the bar of Georgia, the state in which he was born around 1805. He more than likely practiced law in Georgia for a year or so, but by the late 1820s Williamson was a resident of San Felipe de Austin, where empresario Stephen F. Austin maintained his headquarters. Rumor has it that Williamson fought a duel in Georgia over the charms of a certain lady. Although Three-Legged Willie won the contest, the lady in question up and married another gentleman, someone who had not even been a party to the original affair.

Upon Williamson's arrival in San Felipe, he took up residence with such future Texian notables as Ben Milam, Gail Borden (of canned milk fame), and Francis Johnson. A few years down the road, another luminary joined the group, one who would be martyred at the Alamo in March 1836—William Barrett Travis. Many of these new arrivals boarded in the Whiteside Hotel, the tallest structure in town at a story and a half. The inn was owned and operated by James Whiteside.

Not long after his arrival in Texas, Williamson established a newspaper, the *Cotton Plant,* in partnership with Godwin B. Cotten.

Williamson served as editor for the paper from 1829 to 1831. Later, he held the same position for two other area newspapers, the *Texas Gazette* and the *Mexican Citizen.* Cotten had previous newspaper experience, having been publisher of the *Louisiana Gazette* in New Orleans (1815) and the *Mobile Gazette* in Alabama (1816–19). According to *The New Handbook of Texas,* Cotten offered to "publish in his paper all orders, decrees, and advertisements of the *ayuntamiento* [municipal government] of San Felipe in return for two town lots."

The *Texas Gazette* was the colony's first printed newspaper; it was published between 1829 and 1832, first in San Felipe and later in Brazoria. The three contributors to the op-ed page were Cotten, Williamson, and Stephen F. Austin. Cotten disagreed with Austin on many issues of the day, especially the question of Mexican rule. Williamson, although clearly on Cotten's side, attempted to mediate their differences. The *Mexican Citizen* replaced the *Texas Gazette* in 1831 as an organ for the Texians in Austin's colony. Coeditor with Williamson was John Aitken. The historical record is unclear, but Austin may have had input on selection of the newspaper's name. The empresario was determined to foster good relations with Mexico City, an effort even he aborted in time. He believed the newspaper could bode well for the settlers and put a positive light on the hopes and aspirations of Texians toward their Mexican benefactors. Williamson did not agree with Austin's endeavor to curry favor with Mexican authorities. Their differences could have been the reason Williamson soon sold his interest in the *Citizen* to Cotten; Williamson then retired from the newspaper business.

Austin had always been a diehard supporter of coexistence with Mexican authorities. He learned Spanish, considered himself and the colonists Mexican citizens, and saw no reason to upset the status quo. Although not as devoted as Austin to the cause, Williamson did initially support cooperation with Mexico and the concept of Mexican citizenship, an idea that few colonists felt strongly about but went along with for settlement reasons. Then the Mexican government enacted a law that it felt was in Mexico's interest—and it was. The Law of April 6, 1830, lanced the boil of seething resentment that had been festering in many of the colonists.

The law expanded and opened trade outlets for the colonies, which was a positive development. Three other features of the edict,

R. M. WILLIAMSON.

"Robert M. 'Three-Legged Willie' Williamson" portrait

however, set in motion actions that eventually led to that fateful day in April 1836, when on the plain at San Jacinto Texans won the battle that gave them a semblance of independence. The bringing of slaves into Texas was forbidden; contracts with empresarios were apparently terminated; and the detested Article 11 meant to limit or stop altogether the immigration of more settlers from the United States. After the law's implementation, even Austin found his optimism about Mexico City diminished, and Williamson became an outspoken critic of Mexican intentions and actions.

In 1830 Williamson was elected *sindico procurador* (city attorney) for the *ayuntamiento*. He defeated his opponent, Stephen Richardson, 250 to 60 votes. This was a longstanding Spanish position, and it afforded the Texian the opportunity to become familiar with the inner workings of local Mexican officialdom.

In 1832 Williamson was brought into the fray of the Anahuac Disturbance. Situated on Trinity Bay some eighty miles east of San Felipe, Anahuac had a Mexican army force commanded by the egotistical and dictatorial Colonel John Davis Bradburn. The commander heard rumors that Anglos, both foreign and domestic, were going to attack the port under his protection. He believed that Travis and lawyer Patrick C. Jack were instigators and arrested them. Three-Legged Willie headed a contingency of Texians to free the two men. After double-crossing the rebels, Bradburn was relieved of his command by Mexican authorities; Travis and Jack were freed.

The Texians held a deep hatred for Bradburn, a Virginian by birth who had joined filibuster activities in the early 1800s when Mexico was fighting Spain for independence. Adept at choosing the right side in politics, he bent with the wind and remained in the Mexican army. Bradburn had no qualms about fighting fellow Anglos in the ensuing years. Even after being ousted at Anahuac, he stayed active in Mexican governmental and military affairs until his death in April 1842 in Matamoras, Mexico.

Three-Legged Willie felt the wrath of the Mexican government fall on him. Due to his action against Mexican authorities in the Anahuac Disturbance and his continual anti-Mexican pronouncements, both oral and written, Mexico City issued an arrest order for Williamson and several others in July 1835. Williamson avoided capture by hiding out in Mina (today's Bastrop).

Williamson's peace and quiet in Mina was short lived. In October a cadre of some 180 Mexican cavalry showed up at Gonzales, south of San Antonio, demanding that the Texians turn over a specific cannon in their possession. Mexican authorities had originally given the cannon to the townspeople to aid in their fight against area Indians. With tension running high between the colonists and Mexican authorities, the latter had no desire to let such a powerful weapon remain in the hands of the rebels.

Once again, Williamson was in the thick of things. He was in the group that rolled the cannon into full view of the soldiers standing on the opposite side of the Guadalupe River. Willie is credited with devising the slogan COME AND TAKE IT. According to author Duncan W. Robinson, "This challenge . . . became the fighting sentence woven a little later into the first Texas Revolutionary battle flag."

As for the Mexican soldiers, when bullets from Texian guns started hitting the ground around them, they turned toward San Antonio Road. After a day of scuffles between the two belligerents, the Mexicans returned to the site of the Alamo.

A strong advocate for Texas independence, Williamson campaigned for Texians to stand up against "Mexican tyranny." He had used his newspaper as a focal point for pronouncements against the dictatorial laws and attitudes coming out of Mexico City. This stand, of course, had put him at odds with Austin, but the two had managed to stay on amiable terms. Well educated, vocal in his beliefs, and a leader in his bailiwick, Williamson was elected a representative to the Consultation, a quorum of Texians who met to discuss prerevolutionary disagreements with Mexico. (They used the term "consultation" because it seemed less belligerent than "convention.")

The Consultation met on November 11, 1835, in San Felipe. The Austin faction, outnumbered at the meeting, favored a hand for harmony with their benefactors; the group led by John A. Wharton and Henry Smith was on the opposite side. Unwilling to call an out-and-out "to arms" for independence, members of the Consultation did what most governmental units do—formed another committee.

Members of the Consultation organized and set in motion a provisional government in anticipation of eventually becoming an independent country. The provisional government served as the only official forum in Texas from November 15, 1835, to March 1, 1836, although it was about as inactive as a functionary could be. Internal differences and personality conflicts virtually ended the provisional unit by the first part of February 1836.

On November 28, 1835, officials of the government pro tem appointed Williamson to the rank of major, with his first duty being to organize a cadre of Rangers. William H. Arrington, Isaac W. Burton, and John J. Tumlinson were appointed to the rank of captain to serve under Williamson. How well this fits into Texas history: The first major leader of one of the best-known law enforcement agencies in America was disabled. Yet the notion of being handicapped probably never crossed Williamson's mind.

Before Williamson could complete the Ranger chore, more pressing events took place. After the Battle of the Alamo in March 1836, General Sam Houston, his army, and civilians fled east in what became known as the Runaway Scrape, staying ahead of Santa Anna's approaching army. Houston ordered that nothing useful be left behind for the Mexicans, so a scorched-earth policy was implemented in the Texians' wake. The Rangers were called in to protect the rear of the Runaway Scrape and to ensure that citizens were moved out quickly and safely. Captain Tumlinson and Lieutenant Jo Rodger were given permission to leave the Rangers so they might tend to their families during those hectic days. Williamson assumed their positions.

Little more than a month later, Texians gained their freedom in a fierce, bloody, but extremely short battle at San Jacinto. The Rangers, as a unit, did not participate in the battle. They were based on the western frontier, assigned to deter any uprising by Indians. Indians were quiet during the Texas-Mexico upheaval, and so the Rangers had few disturbances to quell. Some individuals who later became well-known Rangers did serve at San Jacinto. Williamson participated as a private in William H. Smith's cavalry unit, although the roster of combatants lists him as W. W. Williamson. As a show of his open disdain for Santa Anna's army, Three-Legged Willie wore a coonskin cap, reminiscent of that worn by Davy Crockett, but with nine tails attached.

In recognition of his service, Williamson received a certificate of land grant dated May 26, 1838, and signed by Charles Mason, secretary of war for the Republic of Texas. The grant consisted of "640 acres of donation land, in accordance with an act of congress passed on 21 December 1837, for having fought at San Jacinto."

With a tenuous peace following the Battle of San Jacinto and a semblance of independence, the Republic of Texas turned to matters of organization. Williamson's tenure with the Rangers was short lived. On December 16, 1836, the First Congress of the Republic appointed him judge of the third judicial district. With this appointment he automatically became a member of the supreme court of the Republic of Texas.

The settlement of Columbus, in present-day Colorado County, was one victim of Sam Houston's scorched-earth policy. When Williamson arrived to open the first session of the district court on the site in early 1837, there was not a building left standing suitable for conducting the court's business. Not to be deterred, Judge Williamson set up a table and opened court under a large oak tree. (Some four months later, the county courthouse was erected on an adjacent lot.)

Williamson's star continued to rise. He represented Washington County in the House of Representatives in the Republic's Fifth, Sixth, and Seventh Congresses. The Eighth Congress found him in the Senate and the Ninth back in the House. Through some controversy, Williamson lost his seat in the Eighth session.

According to publisher J. Marvin Hunter, in a July 1928 edition of the *Frontier Times,* Williamson earned an enviable reputation for his "splendid bursts of eloquence, his withering sarcasm and ridicule, his keen sense of humor that often destroyed an adversary with a single shaft, his absolute freedom from fear, and his unwavering honesty" while serving in the Republic's Congress.

Three-Legged Willie was as strong in his advocacy for Texas annexation as he had been for Texas independence. This fervor was exemplified when he named one of his sons Annexus. Following annexation in 1845, citizens of the new state elected Williamson to public office during the first two legislatures.

By then Williamson had become quite well known for his courtroom pronouncements. The judge sentenced one man to be hanged the day after his trial ended. A petition signed by citizens and even members of the jury, asking for a delay in carrying out the sentence, could not persuade the judge to do so. As author John Q. Anderson relates, "The Judge replied to the petition that the man had been found guilty, the jail was very unsafe, and . . . uncomfortable. He did not think any man ought to be required to stay in it any longer than was necessary. The man was hung!"

On another occasion Williamson set his judicial paraphernalia on a table and laid a rifle and a pistol in plain view. Then he gaveled the room to order and, letting those present know that he would brook no interference in his proceedings, announced, "Hear ye, hear ye, court for the Third District is either now in session or—somebody's going to get killed." Needless to say, the session moved on without hindrance.

Judges as well as lawmen had to be tough on the early Texas frontier. Williamson proved he had the mettle to do his job. This mettle came in handy when he had to conduct court in Shelby County in 1837, a county in which the people decreed that no court was to be held. The general feeling was that most of the male residents had at one time or another probably committed some crime. In addition, it would have been difficult to find jurors honest enough—and brave enough—to testify in open court.

There being no proper judicial accoutrements, the judge reportedly drew up a dry-goods box for his bench and gaveled the court to order. A lawyer by the name of Charlton rose and read a decree to the judge. When Williamson inquired by what authority the resolution was enacted, Charlton placed a Bowie knife on the table in front of the judge and answered, "This is the statute which governs in such cases." With steady eyes fixed on the lawyer, Williamson pulled a pistol from his person and pointed it at Charlton. Slowly but menacingly, the judge said, "And this is the constitution which overrides the statute." The trial continued without further incident. There are several versions of the confrontation, but all show Williamson's lack of fear and his determination to enforce the rule of law.

In another legendary story Williamson sentenced a prisoner to a long time in jail. The crime the man committed was particularly brutal, and the judge let the expletives flow during the sentencing phase of the trial. The prisoner resented the judge's language and challenged him: "Judge, you can sit on the bench and use strong language toward me because I am unarmed and in shackles." It is easy to imagine the hush that fell over the courtroom, especially when Three-Legged Willie temporarily adjourned court, stepped from behind the bench, and had the prisoner's shackles removed. The judge looked him in the eye and said, "Shoot." The prisoner made no effort to comply with the judge's directive.

Williamson came by his tenacity and bravado naturally. His grandfather attained the rank of colonel under George Washington, and his father marched forth during the War of 1812.

As author Bob Bowman reports, not even arson could deter Williamson from carrying out his judicial duties. When the judge arrived in one community to convene court only to find that the courthouse had been burned down intentionally, he set up shop in the local schoolhouse. The case before the court involved horse thieves. The defense attorney challenged the charges against his clients, pointing out that all evidence against them had burned in the fire. Williamson calmly reached into his coat pocket and pulled out copies of the charges and the warrants. The trial proceeded.

Three-Legged Willie's feelings toward American Indians are unknown, but Bowman again provides insight into the judge's character with the following tale. Williamson once rode into a town just in time to stop a mob from hanging an Indian accused of raping a white woman. The judge ordered the victim jailed and set trial for the following day. During the trial the truth came out: The Indian had simply walked into town to buy tobacco. The story was that a Comanche had killed the accuser's brother, and she was seeking revenge on all Indians. There had been no rape. Bowman states that Williamson not only cleared the Indian, but also "ordered the woman's husband to buy the Indian all the tobacco he could chew."

The judge showed unusual fairness in the incident. He had lived on the edge of Indian problems in Bastrop, had been engaged in several fights with the natives, and was acquainted with many Indian fighters of the day. He also knew Josiah Wilbarger, one of the few frontiersmen to survive scalping.

In his spare time Williamson was an accomplished musician, especially with the banjo. His wooden leg came in handy at fandangos and barn dances, by beating time to the music as he sang and played his fiddle. The ever-active and versatile judge expanded his abilities into teaching school, sitting in front as the class members read aloud from their books. His rapturous speech also brought him to the pulpit, where he often gave Sunday sermons. The judge was no saint, however. He did some carousing but kept it within the bounds of propriety. Once, following a night of jocularity, he broke his wooden leg. He showed up at the home of his close friend Noah Smithwick, woke up the soundly sleeping blacksmith, and asked him to fix the damaged limb. Soon Williamson was on his merry way.

Despite Williamson's role in Texas's fight for independence and annexation, and his government service in elected office and in the judiciary, the fickleness of his constituents came through. He was defeated in his run for Congress in 1850, and his candidacy for lieutenant governor in 1851 failed. Consequently, Three-Legged Willie retired from public office.

On the 640 acres of land that the judge received for participating in the battle of San Jacinto, he had established a plantation near the small community of Independence, Washington County, and settled down with his family. (He was married to Mary Jane Edwards, daughter of Gustavus E. Edwards, one of Stephen F. Austin's Old Three

Hundred.) After retirement Williamson turned to homeschooling his children and compiling material pertaining to the events leading up to the Texas Revolution. Because he was on the cusp of such events, his thoughts and experiences would have been invaluable to future historians.

Unfortunately, in 1857 Williamson was struck by an unrecorded ailment that affected his mental well-being. His wife's death in 1858 dashed any hope of his spirit rebounding, and the following year, on December 22, he passed away at the relatively young age of fifty-four. He was living with his father-in-law in Wharton when the end came. Williamson's body was moved to the state cemetery in Austin in 1930, and the state placed a memorial at his gravesite.

In early 1848 residents of western Milam County petitioned the legislature in Austin to organize a new county. In those days of slow and often difficult travel, Milam residents had to spend several days on the road to reach the county courthouse some fifty or so miles away. A couple of names suggested for the new county were San Gabriel and Clear Water. The legislature accepted the petition and organized a new county but christened it for Robert McAlpin Williamson.

Many historians believe that Williamson has never received his due as an important figure in Texas history. On March 21, 1891, state senator George Clark of Waco delivered a long and flowery oration while dedicating a painting of Judge Williamson that was to hang in the Senate chambers. Clark commented, "Robert M. Williamson had done as much, if not more, than any other man in precipitating and sustaining the revolution of 1835–1836 . . . With a price on his head, that beckoned no quarter if captured . . . As an object of special vengeance by [Mexico], he faced the storm, defied the tyrant, and redoubled his efforts to free his country, knowing that his good life would be the penalty for a failure."

Williamson made a strong case for his legacy in the epitaph that he wrote for himself: "I have lived in Texas near thirty years, and in that time I have rendered all the service in my power, so help me God—and my only regret is that in the darkest hours I could then do no more for her."

Three-Legged Willie was, by all accounts, an outstanding example of honesty and integrity. The Honorable George Clark of Waco, Texas, deemed the man "an upright and honest judge who unflinchingly administered the law." Although he was in a position to accumulate great wealth, "it may be stated as creditable to his integrity that in the midst of corruption and speculation he lived and died in poverty."

Few of us can expect a better epitaph.

11

Madam Candelaria

WAS SHE AT THE ALAMO—OR WASN'T SHE?

On March 6, 1836, the final assault by the Mexican army on the Alamo took place. For thirteen days, anywhere from fifteen hundred to six thousand troops (the figures vary) led by General Antonio López de Santa Anna had laid siege to the crumbling San Antonio mission. The Alamo, manned by some 182 Texians, defended a target of little military importance and gave their lives for their action. Santa Anna brought about the deaths of hundreds of Mexican soldiers more for vanity's sake than for a viable military victory.

The bodies of the 182 Texians were stacked like cordwood and burned. Many of the Mexican dead were burned, but there were so many that the bulk had to be thrown into the San Antonio River. The bloated bodies soon created a stench that covered the city and caused many residents to become ill.

The Daughters of the Republic of Texas (DRT) lists about eighteen survivors of the Alamo; these men acted as courtiers and foragers. An unknown number of black slaves also walked away from the siege unscathed. The other survivors were family members taken into the mission prior to the battle in a misguided attempt to save them from the Mexican army. Santa Anna released these women and children, not through any benevolence on his part, but because he wanted them to spread word about the devastation wrought on the Alamo. This was a warning of what lay in store for anyone defying the Mexican government.

The best-known of the Alamo survivors, at least historically, were Susanna Dickinson and her young daughter, Angelina. Others included Francisco Esparza, Gertrudis Navarro, Petra Gonzales, and Concepión Losoya and her son, Juan—all family members of Mexican or Tejano defenders of the Alamo. Many of the children lived into the twentieth century, married, and had offspring of their own. Imagine the stories they must have told their grandchildren!

One name missing from the DRT list of survivors is Andrea Castañón Villanueva, a woman known as Madam Candelaria. As with so many early Texas residents, Andrea had much mystique in her background. She sometimes claimed to have been born in Laredo, Texas, in November 1785, to Antonio Castañón and Francisca Ramírez. Her father was a Spanish soldier who saw service in Cuba and later transferred to the remote frontier to fight Indians; her mother was Mexican. At other times she listed San Juan Bautista, near present-day Eagle Pass, Texas, as her place of birth. Some researchers say that she was born across the border, in Presidio del Rio Grande, and that her parents moved to Laredo when Andrea was about three years old.

When Andrea was a young woman, she moved to San Antonio, where she served as a cook in the household of Gertrudis Pérez Cordero, wife of the governor of Texas and Coahuila. At an early but unknown age, Andrea married Silberio Flores y Abrigo, a follower of Father Miguel Hidalgo and his Mexican rebellion against Spain. Flores died in battle against Spanish Royalists at Medina River, near San Antonio.

To the victor go the spoils, and the Spanish were not tolerant conquerors. They arrested many of the men of San Antonio and

Madam Candelaria

confined them in suffocating, windowless buildings. A great number succumbed to the heat and lack of air. The women were forced to spend hours on their knees at *metates* (grinding stones), making tortillas for the victorious soldiers. The Spanish returned to Mexico in the spring of 1814.

When Andrea was in her forties, she married Candelario Villanueva. Andrea and Candelario parented four children. Being of a benevolent nature, she also raised twenty-two orphans. On one occasion the court in San Antonio received a petition regarding custody of an abused child. The judge asked if, with remuneration from the court, Andrea would be willing to take the child. She agreed but refused any payment, instead insisting that she be allowed to adopt the waif; the adoption was approved. Her station in life must have been one of affluence because she became a sort of traveler's aid, coming to the financial rescue of many strangers stranded in San Antonio. She also extended help to the poor and performed other deeds of mercy, often serving as a nurse to the local citizenry.

Andrea's services were especially in demand when San Antonio was hit by cholera and typhoid during a three-year period beginning in 1819, and again during a smallpox epidemic several decades later.

Andrea was vivacious and outgoing. Typical of the Mexican character, she was an accomplished cook and excellent hostess. San Antonio today hosts many festivals; in Andrea's time the city saw even more. The most popular festival of the day was the fandango dancing extravaganza, a Castilian tradition held over from Spanish rule. Biographer Leticia Neva described Andrea at the 1986 Battle of Flowers Speech Tournament as a woman "with bright eyes and extraordinary activity, [who] became the presiding genius of the fandangos. She prepared many delicious dishes for the people, and soon became known as the 'patroness of the fandango.'"

Andrea might have passed through history remembered by a few as a kind and generous soul. Her tombstone would, by now, probably be covered with weeds or so eroded that the etching would be almost illegible, but for one thing: Andrea claimed that she was a survivor of the Alamo battle and that she had, in fact, nursed James Bowie, who was suffering from typhoid or tuberculosis at the time of the fight. (Bowie, a brawler for all seasons, had acquired his notoriety in September 1827 when, with his ferocious namesake knife, he sliced a man to death on a river sandbar near Natchez, Mississippi.)

Many historians accept her claim. Although none of the other Alamo survivors attested to seeing her at the battle site, only one denied that it was possible. In a May 1907 interview, Enrique Esparza adamantly rejected the idea that Madam Candelaria was in the Alamo at the time of the battle. Enrique was a young boy during the siege; his memory may have dimmed with the passage of time.

His doubts aside, most of the people of her time accepted Madam Candelaria's claim. After all, she had demonstrated her compassion and generosity for many years. Why would she not carry the same feelings into the Alamo? And the state of Texas believed her, going so far as to grant her a pension of $12 a month for being a survivor of the Alamo and for aiding victims of smallpox in and around San Antonio.

The pension bill passed the state legislature on February 12, 1891, and became effective April 13, 1891. No substantiating reports or testimony were required, and the normal three-day reading for such bills was waived. A petition by the Alamo Monument Association of San Antonio backed Madam Candelaria's claim and helped secure passage of the bill.

Several legendary Texians had already spoken in support of Madam Candelaria. John "Rip" Ford, a renowned Texas Ranger who at the time was Deputy Collector of Internal Revenue in San Antonio, wrote a letter to Governor Lawrence Sullivan Ross on her behalf. The letter, dated March 15, 1889, asked the governor to urge the legislature to approve a pension for Candelaria. Ford claimed that her services at the Alamo, as well as her attention to the needs of Anglos and her fellow Mexicans in San Antonio, warranted such consideration. The letter contained the signatures of twenty-six supporters, including such well-known individuals as General Hamilton Bee, businessman Sam Maverick Jr., and Mary Maverick, a long-serving president of the Alamo Monument Association.

Why would Andrea walk into the Alamo at that most precipitous time, putting her life on the line as well as flaunting her government? What would cause her to sacrifice what was evidently a solid, secure standing in San Antonio to oppose the forces of Santa Anna? Maybe she was honoring the memory of her first husband, who met his fate in 1813 during the Mexican Revolution. More than likely, it was out of friendship for Sam Houston and James Bowie, as well as her deep feeling for freedom fighters.

Let us go back to the days before the Battle of the Alamo, to examine how those friendships led her to the ill-fated fort. Andrea had opened an inn near Alamo Plaza during the 1830s. This was a dynamic time in Tejas, more dynamic than anyone realized. Mexico had gained its independence from Spain in 1821 and soon after opened the borders of its northern province to the Americans. There was at least a twofold purpose behind this action, a move that seemed reasonable at the time but later was regretted. First, Mexico wanted a limited number of American settlers to serve as a buffer against full movement into its empire. Second, and just as important, officials in Mexico City saw how the Anglos were handling their Indian problem; maybe they could do the same with the hostile forces wreaking havoc on Mexican villages and their citizens.

The Anglos that crossed the Red and Sabine Rivers were a curious lot. They accepted the requirement of becoming Mexican citizens matter-of-factly. They were there for land, not governmental loyalties. They gave only lip service to the mandatory conversion to the Catholic faith. But they had an innate trait that suggested the events to come. These new "Mexicans" were the descendants of fathers and mothers who had fought the British for independence. The War of 1812 and innumerable Indian conflicts had hardened them. War did not frighten them; the absence of independence did. This absence they found in their new home, a land ripe for rebellion—and they were the ones to foment the uprising.

Not only *Norte Americanos* were repulsed at the heavy-handed and dictatorial actions coming out of Mexico City. Such notable Mexican Tejanos as Jose Navarro, Lorenzo de Zavalos, Placido Benavides, and the father-and-son team of Erasmo and Juan Seguin convened with the Anglos to chart the future course of Tejas.

Andrea heard all the plotting and planning. Long a supporter of those desiring freedom, she listened intently to the words passing between this band of disparate but like-thinking men. She became more intrigued with the men and their ideas upon the arrival on the scene of David "Davy" Crockett. This tall, well-built man captivated her. He was jolly on the outside, with a will of iron racing through his soul. Although Andrea was awestruck by the presence of the Tennessean, Sam Houston was the person who persuaded her to enter the Alamo as Mexican troops appeared on the southern horizon.

The commander of the Texian army, such as it was, did not want to waste men or material defending the Alamo, a task he correctly considered useless. Once Bowie, Crockett, William Travis, and the others decided to remain in place despite his orders, Houston attempted to support and reinforce them, to little avail. When he learned that

Bowie had been injured and was suffering from respiratory ailments, Houston inveighed upon Andrea to tend to the warrior. The extent of Bowie's injuries and illnesses, and the cause of them, is open to historical speculation.

Andrea was a *curandero,* a Mexican folk healer, part shaman, part herbalist, part psychiatrist, who specialized in medieval Spanish medicine and [Indian] remedies. Anglo doctors were available in the Alamo, but medicines were virtually nil. Houston asking Andrea to help Bowie was an attempt to do all possible for the soldier. Since Bowie had married into a Mexican family of high standing prior to entering the Alamo and spoke fluent Spanish, he was familiar with the cultural influence of the *curandero.*

If Andrea performed as similar healers of the day did, she treated Bowie by bribing the spirits with brightly colored gadgets. A more distasteful practice was that of rubbing an egg over Bowie, then cracking open the egg so she could read the cause of the illness.

Bowie realized his illnesses were probably contagious and had his person moved from the officers' quarters to the barracks of the enlisted troops. Although Andrea agreed to aid Bowie as best she could, his move to the enlisted quarters placed her in a quandary. The barracks, called the "gamblers' den" by those in the compound, would discredit her upstanding reputation in the community. A woman of her station could not afford to be caught anywhere near such a notorious place.

Finally accepting her responsibility to Bowie and to Houston, Andrea took a drastic step, one that allowed her to both meet her obligation and preserve her social standing. When she walked through the door of the enlisted quarters, at age fifty-three, she left Andrea Villanueva outside. While attending to her patient, she would be known as Madam Candelaria, apparently a feminization of her husband's name, Candelario. Henceforth, Madam Candelaria would be a recognizable name around San Antonio, especially after the Alamo conflict.

From the time the Alamo ceased to be a battleground until her death, Andrea told and retold her version of the five days she spent inside the mission, the fifth day being the fatal March 6, 1836. She told of Travis drawing a line in the sand and asking those who were willing to accept death, their certain fate at the Alamo, to step over the line. She recalled Bowie, lying on his cot, telling the men to carry him across. She said that Louis "Moses" Rose refused to remain behind the walls and escaped from the confines of the mission.

The matter of the line in the sand (more likely in dirt) has tormented historians for more than 170 years. While most writers reject the idea as nothing more than embellishment of a saga that needs no embellishment, Madam Candelaria attested that she witnessed the act. Her presence at the Alamo may have been in question, but that of Susanna Dickinson was not. In 1881, some forty-five years following the day she walked out of the ruins of that old, pockmarked sanctuary, Susanna paid her first return visit to the grounds of the Alamo. Followed by a reporter from the *San Antonio Daily Express*, she retold the story of Travis and the line he drew with his saber.

Why is it so difficult to believe that Travis would make such a gesture? He was certainly a flamboyant individual, given to a flair for the dramatic, such as the firing of the cannon as a reply to Santa Anna's demand for surrender. But the best examples of his exuberance were his appeals for help in defending the Alamo. Only someone with a sense of histrionics and posterity could have written such phrases as "I shall have to fight the enemy on his own terms," "[T]he victory will cost the enemy so dear, that it will be worse for him than defeat," and "God and Texas, Victory or Death."

According to Madam Candelaria, Crockett loaded two pistols and placed them on the cot beside Bowie. She also said that her patient, on his deathbed, fought until the very end, that he killed at least two Mexican soldiers before being bayoneted to death and carried out by his attackers. More than one source puts Bowie's death at least six hours before Santa Anna's final assault. This is another question mark in Candelaria's story.

The soldiers supposedly wounded her with bayonets as many as seven times when she pleaded with them not to murder a sick man. She displayed the wounds proudly as she relayed her experiences. But Madam Candelaria seldom repeated the same version twice when she told her story. For some historians this inconsistency puts her claims in doubt.

There are also questions as to how Crockett met his end. Many say that the Tennessean surrendered and was executed soon thereafter. Madam Candelaria offered a different version of his last moments, as quoted by columnist Kent Biffle in the *Dallas Morning News,* "I could never regard Crockett as a hero until I saw him die. He looked grand and terrible standing at the doorway of the church and swinging something bright over his head . . . A heap of dead was piled at his feet, and the Mexicans were lunging at him with bayonets, but he would not retreat an inch. Crockett fell and the Mexicans poured into the Alamo."

Thus Madam Candelaria declared herself an eyewitness to the last moments of Crockett's life and the valor he exhibited. In an interview many years after the battle, Susanna Dickinson verified Andrea's version. Susanna did not see the final assault, but within minutes of the last surge, she was walking the terrain filled with dead bodies. She said that a pile of corpses was being burned and she recognized the odd cap that Crockett wore lying on the ground next to the pyre.

After the Battle of the Alamo, Madam Candelaria remained in San Antonio and continued her charitable deeds and other good works. As time passed and her renown began to spread, people from all over the country and from all walks of life visited her in the small house at 419 South Concho Street where she lived with her daughter, Mrs. Francisca Flores Pacheco. Andrea became the object of photographers and autograph hounds, much like celebrities of today. The fame was to her liking. She relished the attention and loved telling her stories over and over.

The controversy over whether Andrea was in the Alamo at the time of the battle occupies only a minute space in the recordings of Texas history. No one verified that she was at the site in March 1836; no one verified that she was not. However, Susanna Dickinson did counter Andrea's claim by calling her a "fraud." In rebuttal Madam Candelaria termed Susanna "a racist who hated Mexicans."

One of the reasons Madam Candelaria's stories are so hard to believe is that they varied so much with each of her tellings. She said that Susanna and Almeron, her husband, had a son and that during the final siege of the Alamo, Almeron came to the chapel, picked up his son, strapped the boy to his chest, and went back to the battle. Both were soon killed. There is no evidence that Susanna ever gave birth to a boy. Her only child was a girl, Angelina. Renditions like this throw doubt on Madam Candelaria's other ramblings.

Moreover, she offered great detail on the final assault on March 6—the positions of the Mexican troops, the firepower on both sides, and the order in which the defenders were killed. If she was, by her own words, confined to a small room while nursing Bowie, it is difficult to understand how she could have observed so much over those last two or three hours.

It is doubtful that the full truth of Madam Candelaria's experience will ever be known. But as time goes on, the questions become less important. Madam Candelaria's benefit to society far outweighs any doubts about her presence in that fateful, crumbling building more than 170 years ago.

Madam Candelaria lived a full life. In her final days a Mexican hairless dog was her constant companion, and she reputedly credited the animal with helping ease her arthritic pain. The *curandero* passed away when old age (or the grippe) took her on February 10, 1899, at the age of 113. She was interred in San Fernando Cemetery in San Antonio, the city that brought her so much fame.

12

James Briton Bailey

HE'S STILL LOOKING FOR HIS JUG

Most of the early settlers in Mexican Texas came to make a new life for themselves and their families. They quietly went about the drudgery of breaking ground for farming, fought Indians, and tended to family illnesses and the myriad of other events of the day. These are the people you seldom read about. Then along comes an individual like Brit Bailey to roil the peace. Boisterous, always looking for a fight, an Amazon of a man, he made his own reputation, which would be in conflict with the quieter, more self-involved settlers in the area. Brit was an ex-convict; restless, industrious, and very independent. And how many people would make a man of the cloth undress (under threat of a rifle) and do a dance? Brit would—and did. Brit was cut from a different swath of cloth. And he liked it and wanted it that way.

Born on August 1, 1779, in North Carolina, Brit was the son of Kenneth Bailey, who claimed lineage from Scotland's famed royal Robert the Bruce, once a king of Scotland. Brit and his first wife, Edith Smith, had six children. When Edith passed away around 1815, Brit married her sister, Nancy (also known as Dorothy or Dot). She and Brit parented five additional offspring. Some of Brit's children, from what

136

is known of them, suffered untimely deaths. James drowned in a river at a very young age; Indians slew Phelps; and Smith met his demise at the Battle of the Alamo. Brit's daughter Mary, however, apparently had a happy life and married an Old Three Hundred settler by the name of Joseph Henry Polley. Her sister Betsey was captured by Indians but somehow managed to escape.

Brit moved his wife, Edith, and their six children to Kentucky, where they lived for a few years. Little is known of Brit's life in North Carolina, but his reputation as a hell-raiser with questionable ethics emerged during his brief stay in the Bluegrass State. Reports have it that he was elected to the Kentucky legislature, but he might have been brought up on charges—and found guilty—of forgery. This situation probably prompted his relocation south, to Tennessee. Sometime amid all this moving around, Brit managed to serve in the War of 1812.

Wanderlust was very much a part of Brit's persona. Too, with his abrasive personality, he found it difficult to cultivate friends. The flowery words covering the country about the land west of the Sabine appealed to someone of Brit's character. Freedom, law virtually unknown, land for the taking—these things were all magnets for a man with a large family and an independent mind, always willing to take chances. And so without another thought, Brit posted the GTT (Gone to Texas) sign on his cabin door, gathered his clan, and moved out.

As many before him had done, Brit chose water travel from New Orleans as the quickest, easiest, and safest mode of travel to his destination. After weeks driving oxen and horses from Tennessee, along muddy paths and through thick forests, Brit, his family, and half a dozen adult slaves arrived in the Crescent City. Coming at a most opportune time, they were able to book passage on a ship

Illustration of Brit Bailey by Ann Brightwell

almost immediately. The 150-mile journey was an enjoyable one for the adults, but confining and potentially boring for the children. Pirate Jean Lafitte had made Galveston his headquarters at the time, so the ship's crew kept the children enthralled with pirate stories.

Brit and his entourage landed on what is today Galveston Island. The year was 1818 (a more exact date is unknown). Securing a new stock of oxen and wagons, Brit loaded up his group, and a few days later they were camping on the Brazos River in East Texas. Brit asserted that he bought the land on which he settled from the Spanish government; no title has ever been found to verify his claim. This lack of title proved troublesome later, when Mexico gained its independence from Spain and took possession of all lands Spain had once possessed. The authorities in Mexico City refused to acknowledge Brit's title. Regardless of the legality of his claim, Brit settled on the land three years before Stephen F. Austin's arrival.

When Austin received the status of empresario from Mexico, his colony included land occupied by Brit and his family. Austin considered Brit a squatter and ordered him off the land and out of the colony. Austin had received vast powers as empresario: His word was law, his actions questionable only by Mexican authorities. He wrote Brit a letter that was, in effect, an eviction notice, and gave him sixty days to vacate the area—family, property, and all. There is speculation that Austin did not like Brit because of his unsavory past.

Austin had never met Brit and knew him only by reputation. He went to face his adversary and remind him of the eviction notice but ran into a large, gruff man wielding a rifle. The two men then exchanged words that must have eased tensions somewhat. The empresario asked if Brit was not an ex-convict, to which Brit replied, in words probably apt to some of today's politicians, "'T'ain't that I'm ashamed of. It's the term I served in the Kentucky legislature which sits heavy on my conscience." His crime was one of forgery, but in Brit's view, it was more revenge than criminal. As with many people of the day, Brit had conflicts with the proliferation of banks and their heavy-handed treatment of citizens.

Regardless of their politeness toward each other, Brit was a hellion and in personality and character was far afield from the calmer, more responsible Austin. But for unknown reasons the empresario changed his mind and on July 7, 1824, recognized Brit's claim. Regardless of the circumstances, Brit had from the outset let both Mexican authorities and Austin know that he would never abandon his land.

Today this land is called Bailey's Prairie. After the grant was settled, a community emerged around Brit's homestead, cattle were run, and some settlers developed sugar plantations. A church was built and, later, a school and additional homes popped up on the surrounding prairie. As for Brit, he eventually acquired land covering much of southeast Texas and was one of the largest cattle ranchers in the colony, based primarily on the sturdy longhorns. His herds ranged as far south as Houston and on to the Gulf coast.

Brit and Austin would never be friends, or even warm acquaintances. But on the frontier, with its sparse Anglo population, they knew they had to work together. Austin used Brit's homestead as a meeting place for colonists from the lower Brazos Valley area. The meeting was called to have the settlers take an oath of loyalty to the Constitution of 1824, in which Mexico outlined the requirements for Anglo settlement in Texas; acceptance of Mexican citizenship was one of the stipulations. As either a gesture of goodwill or recognition of Brit's aggressiveness and military-style discipline, Austin appointed him a lieutenant in the militia. Apparently Brit's demeanor captured the attention of local Mexican officials because, in 1829 José María Viesca, governor of Coahuila and Texas, promoted Brit to the rank of captain.

Brit had seen action in the War of 1812 and was not about to miss any excitement in his new home. By 1824 he was well established on his land grant and operated a store at the homestead. Some Karankawa Indians entered the store on June 22 and demanded that the proprietor sell them ammunition. When the clerk refused, a fight ensued. The Indians soon rode away and headed for their encampment by a small stream in southern Brazoria County. In hot pursuit were Brit and a number of settlers. The following morning, June 22, the settlers attacked the Indians. Both sides suffered casualties, and neither could claim victory. In the end the Indians crossed the San Bernard River, and Brit and his men returned to their homes. The event became known as the Battle of Jones Creek; the stream name honors Randal Jones, who led the settlers' attack.

Another incident in which Brit was involved took place in June 1832 at what was then the port of Velasco. (Today the site is part of Brazosport in southern Brazoria County.) On June 26 a Texas militia led by John Austin (no relation to Stephen) and Henry Smith, and including Brit, sailed down the Brazos River to Brazoria. Their mission was to secure two cannons that the Texians planned to use against Mexican troops at Anahuac. Mexican authorities, growing more and more leery of the Anglo settlers and their rapidly increasing number, had established a port of entry at Velasco and installed a garrison commanded by Colonel Domingo de Ugartechea. It is not clear exactly how many troops were on either side, but it is estimated that between one hundred and one hundred fifty Texians faced a Mexican command of some ninety-one to two hundred men.

Colonel Ugartechea ordered the ship carrying the Texians and the cannons to halt; the militia refused. In what would become recognized as the first military engagement of the Texas Revolution, fighting erupted between the two forces. William James Russell, commander of the schooner *Brazoria,* is thought to have fired the first shot for Texas independence when he sent broadsides into the Mexican post. As a defense against Mexican gunshot, the Texians fashioned shields out of three-inch cypress wood stock. The shields were so heavy that it took at least four men to tote each device, except for strongman Strap Buckner, who carried one by himself. The shields were poor defensive cover and were riddled apart by Mexican gunfire. In fact, the bullets splintered the shield Strap carried so badly that the shards jammed into his head, killing him instantly.

The Texians came out ahead in the battle when the Mexicans ran out of ammunition. The settlers suffered an estimated seven dead and fourteen wounded; three of the injured died later of their wounds. The estimated Mexican casualties were five killed and sixteen wounded. After the cease-fire an honorable truce was agreed upon: Colonel Ugartechea and his officers could retain their arms, and all the Mexican troops were permitted to return to Mexico. The Anglos even provided a ship for their safe return. The Texians sailed north with the cannons. The upheaval that had caused the Anahuac Disturbance had been settled, and the weapons were no longer needed.

Brit took guff from no man. He was a hard drinker and never hesitated to use his fists (even when he had no call to); he made and walked his own path and let the devil take the hindquarter. When one of his horses threw him, leaving him bruised and limping, Brit supposedly retaliated by slitting the horse's throat. Well known for his drinking bouts, he once became so intoxicated that he set fire to all the structures on his property. The lone survivor was the main house.

Despite hard work, hard times, and hard drinking, Brit could get involved in some rather comical situations. One evening when the family was away and Brit was alone except for the slaves, a minister stopped by and asked for lodging for the night. It was customary on the frontier that no visitor be turned away. Had the parson known Brit, perhaps he would have chosen another stopover. Regardless, after the two men had supped and were sitting by the fire, Brit, having bent his elbow several times that evening, picked up his shotgun, aimed it at the minister, and ordered the man to undress. Taken aback by the words of his host but at the same time staring into that potent weapon, the minister complied. He was really shocked at Brit's next instruction: to get on the table and do a juba, a traditional slave dance on Southern plantations. Once Brit considered that the man had danced enough, he lowered his gun and sat back down by the hearth.

The minister dressed and then joined Brit by the fire. After a time he saw that his host was feeling little pain. He reached over, picked up the shotgun, and aimed it straight at Brit. No one knows how well Brit danced the juba, but he and the minister became life-long friends.

Despite his prowess and stamina, Brit was a victim of the scourge of the time, cholera. On December 6, 1832, he breathed his last. Some of Brit's contemporaries attributed his death not to disease but "just plain meanness."

Brit's legend grew more after his death, taking on a life of its own. As the story goes, he left instructions that when he died he was to be buried standing up, because he wanted no one saying, "There lies old Brit Bailey." He wanted the living to not look down on him, but instead to say, "There stands Bailey." He also directed that he be buried "with my face to the setting sun. I have been all my life travel-ing westward and I want to face that way when I die." Abiding by his wishes, his widow ordered that an eight-feet-deep hole be dug and that a special casket be designed. When the preparations were com-plete, she had her slaves and others lower the casket into the grave, with Brit's feet first.

Along with those odd requests, Brit demanded that he be buried with his favorite rifle and pistols and sufficient ammunition. When asked why he wanted all this paraphernalia in his casket, Brit replied, "I am a rude man, and know not whom I may meet in another world. I wish to be prepared, as usual, for all enemies."

Like the pharaohs of old, Brit also wanted something to slake his thirst during his long journey in the hereafter. Therefore, a jug of whiskey was to be placed in the casket at his feet. This request may have gone unfulfilled. Reports have it that Brit's wife refused to allow a jug in the casket. Some say she was convinced to forgo the moonshine by the ministering parson. Others speculate that the jug just up and vanished while the slaves were digging the grave.

Brit was buried somewhere between West Columbia and Angleton, near State Highway 35. There is no grave marker, so his exact final resting place is unknown. A tree of distinct form once marked the gravesite, but storms removed it long ago.

Brit was not soon forgotten. A short time after his death, John and Ann Thomas bought the Bailey homestead. They swore that they saw the specter of Brit floating through the house and that the bedroom suddenly became very cold when the apparition appeared. These instances reportedly took place whether the couple slept in the room separately or together.

The legend continues. A story circulates about the time drillers were working in the area. Their equipment struck ground too close to Brit's grave, and his ghost became angry and caused a gas well blowout.

And then there's the tale of the policeman who, in December 1980, long after Ol' Brit had been laid to rest, sent out a distress call over the car radio. When another officer arrived on the scene, he found the caller lying on the floor of the police car, alive but half scared to death. A pungent odor of gunpowder wafted from inside the cruiser.

The policeman rose from the floor of the vehicle and looked at his fellow officer. He said that he had seen a strange red light bouncing around on the prairie. After he called for backup, the light jumped over a fence and floated to the car. The startled officer fired numerous shots at the apparition before it disappeared into thin air.

Some claim that Brit returns to the prairie every seven years, looking for his whiskey. The general consensus, however, is that his ghost appears much more often. The next time you're driving around the Bailey's Prairie region and it is dark and eerie outside, you might see a strange glow hopping over the countryside. Don't worry about it. That's just Ol' Brit, carrying his lantern and searching for his jug.

Martha White McWhirter

SHE WHO WAS SANCTIFIED

John Wesley, the English-born theologian, founded the Methodist Church in Great Britain and America. He also held articles of faith that would serve many followers and become the basis for the first female communal society established in the United States. These tenets—prayer, Scripture meditation, and Holy Communion—became the guiding path for a nineteenth-century woman named Martha White McWhirter. Not only was Martha unique in her thinking, she also conducted her colony as no other colonizer, before or since.

Martha was born May 17, 1827, in Gainesboro, Tennessee, located northeast of Nashville, near the Kentucky state line. Her parents were farmers. She and George M. McWhirter, a lawyer, farmer, and fellow Tennessean (he hailed from nearby Wilson County) became man and wife in 1845. By 1855 the couple had put down stakes along Salado Creek in Bell County, Texas. And within a decade of that—around 1865, following the Civil War, in which George attained the rank of major—they had resettled in Belton, the county seat. This would be the site of a great metamorphosis for the McWhirter family, especially Martha.

In Belton, George operated a store and owned a flour mill. The McWhirters took part in the religious affairs of the community, assisting in the organization of the Union Sunday School. Although Martha was a Methodist from her Tennessee years, the school was interdenominational. In 1870 a Methodist church was established in Belton, but the McWhirters stayed with the Union School. Martha was active in the prayer program, serving as the leader of a women's prayer group that used the Methodist facility until it was locked out by church officials. After that the group met in the homes of members.

Martha gave birth to twelve children, but fate was not kind to her. Four children had already died by 1866, the year in which Martha saw the demise of her brother along with two more of her children. As often happens in such circumstances, Martha felt that for some reason, God was punishing her by taking away members of her family. The matter worried her to no end, and she finally looked for solace in prayer and meditation. Eleanor James, in her article, "The Santificationists of Belton," wrote that Martha became "convinced that God was chastising her and calling her to take thought of her life and the evils around her."

The search for redemption brought Martha a form of peace. She believed that God had filled her soul with the Holy Spirit, that she had been sanctified (freed from sin through divine grace). When she confessed her revelation to members of the women's prayer group, the civic and social structures of Belton were set for upheaval.

It is possible that Martha's revelation was not only a vision, but also inspiration from a religious sect organized almost one hundred years earlier. "Mother" Ann Lee founded the Shakers in 1772, following the deaths of several of her young children. Martha's earlier life in the eastern United States may well have exposed her to teachings of the Shakers.

Although Martha had no major complaints about her marriage to George, other than his possible dalliance with a servant girl, the same could not be said for the marriages of several women in her prayer group and many in the town. Wives were, all too often, little more than chattel to their husbands. Many women could identify with the saying—if not uttered, at least thought thousands of times—"Texas is heaven for men and dogs, but hell for women and oxen." Women could not own property; a number of them suffered abuse at the hands of their spouses, and the "husband's right in the bedroom" knew few if any limits.

Individually, the wives could not alter the status quo. But like labor unions, together they presented a formidable foe. Also like unions, they needed a leader. Martha McWhirter stepped forward and assumed command, bringing her unorthodox religious views to bear on their lives.

According to *The New Handbook of Texas,* Martha informed her followers that she had had "a revelation in which the sanctified were instructed to separate themselves from the undevout." She told unhappy wives to continue their chores around the house but have as little social contact with their husbands as possible. The women also were to abstain completely from conjugal relations.

The lack of a responsive bedmate was more than the menfolk could take. Things soon became intractable at the homes of Martha's followers, and many of the women moved to the McWhirter homestead. These "Sanctified Sisters" formed the nucleus of the first all-female commune in America.

Although Martha was the acknowledged leader of the Woman's Commonwealth, as the society came to be called, it functioned as a republic. Each member had an equal voice in its operation. The women even established a central treasury. From the outset it seems that the Commonwealth simply evolved without benefit of charter or any real planning. Martha possessed intelligence and charisma, the true ingredients of leadership. The other women of the commune probably recognized this and wisely followed her guidance.

Their husbands, on the other hand, became vehement in their opposition to and hatred for Martha and the emerging commune. They increased the abuse of their wives and even assaulted the house in which Martha and some women and children had taken refuge. Gunfire struck the house on at least one occasion, and some of the good citizens of Belton brought one of Martha's fellow Sisters in for a sanity hearing. Nothing came of the maneuver.

The cards were stacked against the women of the day at almost every turn. One husband attacked his wife for allowing three other women into the house to do laundry. The attack resulted in his wife suffering a gash in her head. The other three women were not pliant and fought the mean-tempered husband. Unbelievably, the husband sued the women and received a $100 judgment from the court ($25 for each woman). The general fund of the commune paid the women's fines.

The local populace supplied the majority of commune members; some eleven families contributed most of the Sisters. But Martha did receive requests for information from people all over America. The Sisters actually paid relocation expenses of a California woman who became a member of the Commonwealth.

Becoming more and more surrounded by women, and with Martha's attention focused on the new arrivals, George decided to move into the attic rooms above his mercantile building. His ongoing relationship with Martha was an oddity, to say the least. They never divorced, though they also never again shared a bed. Despite his opposition to her activities, George stood up for his wife in the face of mounting Belton ridicule.

Martha had brought money into the marriage with George and set about spending it to improve living conditions for the Sisters. She had additional housing constructed on the property—against George's wishes—for some of the women, including Mrs. J. C. Henry, who had been severely abused by her husband. The women did most of the construction work themselves (hiring a carpenter for only one day), and the Henry house was ready for occupancy in less than a week.

George died in 1887 and left his entire estate to Martha. Some residents of Belton attributed his death to the treatment rendered by Martha, an absurd accusation. Under the legal system of the day, George could have stipulated disposal of his assets as he pleased and Martha would have had little recourse. As it were, his will served to increase Martha's treasury, which she used to further the cause of the commune.

The Woman's Commonwealth creed stipulated that the Sisters should never leave the property to call on people in town, although they could receive visitors in the commune hotel or any of their homes. As George lay dying, Martha felt that she should go see him but vowed to do so only if "a divine revelation instructed her accordingly." It did not, and she did not.

Another inheritance came into question when a member of the commune refused to accept a $2,000 life insurance policy left to her by her deceased husband. The woman, Sister Johnson, refused the money because her late husband had been "undevout" and they had not lived as man and wife for some time. Sister Johnson's brother had her committed to an insane asylum. Years passed before Martha was able to prevail upon Texas governor John Ireland to have her freed. He acceded to Martha's request. Sister Johnson earned $90 from her labors while in the asylum and donated the money to the Commonwealth's treasury. Her brother had no hesitancy in taking the $2,000 inheritance for himself.

Courtesy of the collection of the Lena Armstrong Public Library, Belton, Texas

Martha White McWhirter

Martha assumed the position of financial advisor to the group. Under her astute monetary guidance, the organization was a self-sufficient and profitable operation in an amazingly short time. With more than two dozen women and children in the commune, money was a necessity. In those days few women worked outside the home, and for those that did, wages were exceedingly meager. An enterprising group led by an even more enterprising leader, the women set out to become financially independent. They raised chickens and sold eggs, took in laundry, and even went to the woods to gather firewood, which they bought in bulk for 25 cents a cord, cut and hauled, and then sold for $3.00 a cord. Some of the women worked as domestics, cleaning, cooking, and such. One woman was tubercular and could not stand up to the slightest labor. Since it was the credo that all members work, this woman served as a teacher for the Sisters' children. It is easy to understand why the women gained financial independence so quickly.

Ever-expanding financial ventures led to larger ownership of Belton property by the commune. Boardinghouses were established, and a hotel, the Central, opened on May 10, 1886. Plans for a second hotel were made but never brought to fruition. The Sisters supposedly leased and operated two hotels in Waco. Their assets also included three farms on the outskirts of Belton.

The women were not subjected to just work and toil. Each member was assigned tasks that consumed only four hours a day. As author Lindsay Meeks notes, "The rest of the day was dedicated to prayer and to educating themselves and their children." These educational endeavors led to the women becoming adept in making shoes, shoeing horses, and practicing dentistry, to mention a few vocations. The tasks rotated among the Sisters; this allowed commune members to work in all phases of the organization. The group also devoted ample time to expanding their cultural learning and enjoyment. They traveled to Mexico City, New York, San Francisco, and other points to delve into various cultures. During a stay in Washington, D.C., they were so impressed with what the city offered that the women talked about one day moving there.

From the outset the Commonwealth was intended to be a women's commune. However, there was an attempt to bring males into the group. Two men from Scotland, brothers Matthew and David Dow, applied for admittance around January or February of 1880. Their acceptance depended on their willingness to consign themselves to being members only, without trying to control the women. The men agreed, but their membership was short lived. Some male citizens of Belton kidnapped the two Scots, flogged them, and managed to have them committed to an asylum.

The brothers were freed the following day, but they never again attempted to enter the commune. Martha, through the British consul, was probably instrumental in securing the men's release. The Dow brothers eventually returned to Belton and went into the mercantile business. Ironically, it was they who provided laundry equipment for the Central Hotel. Although no men officially became members of the Commonwealth, the Sisters had several in their employ, primarily in the hotel. There is some hint that these male employees were secret members of the Commonwealth.

As they gained financial independence, the women obtained increasingly favorable recognition from the citizens of Belton. The commune contributed funds to attract a railroad to the small town. It was not coincidence that the train station was located across the street from the Central Hotel. Martha was a supporter of the local opera house, even having her name engraved on the building's cornerstone. She also became the first woman elected to the city's Board of Trade (today's chamber of commerce.)

It was through the generosity of the Sanctified Sisters that Belton secured its first book depository. The Sisters maintained a small collection of books in their house. They donated the collection to the city, and that donation served as the catalyst for the first public library in Belton.

The Woman's Commonwealth (also known as the Belton Woman's Commonwealth, the True Church Colony, the Texas Women's

Commonwealth, or "Sentus," a sobriquet levied by local citizens) became so profitable that, in 1899, members sold their Belton holdings, estimated at nearly a quarter million dollars (an enormous sum back then), retired, and moved to Washington, D.C. There they bought property at 1437 Kennesaw Avenue. They paid $23,000 for the house and spent $10,000 on renovations—all in cash, as was their custom. They also purchased a farm in Mount Pleasant, Maryland, northwest of Baltimore, near the Pennsylvania state line. They filed a charter in Washington in 1902, establishing the Woman's Commonwealth of Washington, D.C.

As with any sexually segregated congregation, the demise of the Woman's Commonwealth was foreordained. As time passed the children moved toward greener pastures and the women died off. Following Martha's death on April 21, 1904 (at age seventy-seven), Fannie Holtzclaw assumed leadership of the commune. There were about thirty Sisters in the Commonwealth at that time. The Washington property eventually passed to other hands, and in 1918 the last living commune member, Martha Scheble, died at age 101.

During the four decades or so that the Commonwealth was viable, it attained a maximum membership of fifty. Women desiring membership had to attest to dreams or prayers much as the founder had. Candidates also were required to "have had the second blessing of sanctification," according to author Eleanor James. "That they prayed earnestly for some sign of their sanctification, some direct word from God such as Mrs. McWhirter had received."

The organization received criticism because some people felt it was responsible for separating husbands and wives. Despite what really amounted to sour grapes, no evidence ever came to light that the Sisters committed any crimes, indulged in any shady or immoral activities, or perpetrated any other underhanded shenanigans. And yet the churches of Belton closed their doors to the Sisters and talked badly about them in meetings.

One shadow that did hang over the Commonwealth was the members' disdain for doctors and all medical treatment. Their beliefs may have resulted in the death of a baby. As author Melissa Johnson attests, "Even members' deaths were kept secret as long as possible."

There is a story that, if true, might have Martha believing she possessed more than mortal powers. Johnson goes on to relate that Martha stood on the railing of the balcony of the commune's house and "posed . . . to prove that her faith would protect her against harm." Mouthing a silent prayer, Martha "came sailing over the banister" and landed hard on the ground. A doctor was sent for (over the objections of the members), and his prognosis was simple: She had broken two ribs and both legs.

Were the Sisters of Woman's Commonwealth really sanctified, or were they simply sanctimonious? The state of sanctification is a personal thing and can be confirmed only by the individual, if such assurance can be ascertained even then. It does not seem that the ladies were sanctimonious; they did not preach their beliefs to the townspeople or anyone else unless asked.

Regardless of religious leaning and belief, membership in the Commonwealth was completely understandable, at least for most of the Sisters. The women that chose to leave hearth and home for the commune displayed a courage probably envied by other women in Belton and elsewhere. Being little more than property to men was an onus many women of the day would have liked to shuck off. But, for compelling reasons, most wives would not or could not break the ties that bind.

Oddly, the exception to the Commonwealth's general member type was its founder. Martha was not burdened by an abusive husband, she did not have to rely on George for financial support, and he even stood by her when the two separated and no longer lived under the same roof. Furthermore, he left all his assets to Martha upon his demise. Regardless of Martha's reason for founding the commune—vision, revelation, or influence by Shakers—she accomplished what few other people (men or women) were able to do. Through innate intelligence, charisma, and perseverance, she not only instituted a viable and relatively long-lived commune, but also maintained a cohesive, happy union of members.

Given her position and the fact that she inspired almost absolute devotion from the ladies, Martha could have been a shrew or a dictator. There is no indication that she was either. This daughter of Texas truly earned her place in history.

Milton Faver

THE BARON OF WEST TEXAS

Although Texas was becoming more populated after Stephen F. Austin instituted his Old Three Hundred, the settlers were hesitant about exposing their families and themselves to the hostilities in West Texas. Indians were still causing problems, and the weather and land were inhospitable to the farmer of eastern Texas. Not all people were dissuaded by these foreboding omens. One such individual was Milton Faver, another of those quaint characters that roamed Texas in the 1800s. As with many of his era, there are conflicting stories about his age and place of birth, and much other information and misinformation.

Milton supposedly was born in Virginia around 1822, although Kentucky, Missouri, and far-off New York also have been identified as possible birth sites. His parentage and upbringing are unknown, but he could have carried English or French blood in his veins, as noted by Johnny D. Boggs in *Wild West*. At around age eighteen he was in Missouri, where he fought a duel with a fellow citizen. What brought on the shootout is anyone's guess. Milton won the battle and, thinking he had killed his opponent, decided to flee for friendlier climes.

The year 1840 found him in Mexico. Milton was employed by Francisco De León in Meoqui, about halfway between Chihuahua and the Mexican border town of Ojinaga, across the Rio Grande from Presidio. De León operated a flour mill in Meoqui, and it served as Milton's training ground in Mexican ways. He also learned Spanish, adopted the name Don Melitón, and found a wife—he and Francisca Ramírez married shortly after their first meeting. He was of the Catholic faith, but it is unknown whether it was from his youth or he converted when he married Francisca. (Some say that Milton actually married her sister Josefita first. Here, again, the record is unclear.)

As time would prove, Milton was not one to let grass grow under his feet; nor would he pass his productive time toiling for someone else. He set up a freight business, starting with just one wagon and oxen bearing freight between Meoqui and Ojinaga. A shrewd businessman with an eye for profit, he soon expanded his service to more lucrative routes, namely the Chihuahua and Santa Fe Trails, both of which carried him into American territory. He delivered goods produced in Mexico, sold them along the trails, and then returned to Meoqui with products from the United States.

The Anglos that settled the eastern part of Texas, from the Balcones Fault to the Sabine River, had pretty well reduced the Indian threat by the 1850s. The Indians did not go quietly into the dark night, however. They were still dangerous in sparsely populated West Texas. Milton discovered this fact early in his forays across the big river. He was seriously injured at least once in an Indian attack, and his wagons were under constant threat from both Indians and *bandidos.*

Milton suffered few financial setbacks during his lifetime. The freight business proved so profitable that he turned it over to the people who worked for him and moved his family—his wife and a son, Juan—to the Rio Grande site of Ojinaga. This move probably took

Milton Faver on horseback

place around 1856. Milton opened a store in Ojinaga but remained there only a year at most. He later moved some twenty-five miles north of the Rio Grande into Texas. He put down stakes at the Chinati mountain range in Presidio County, between the towns of Presidio and Marfa. He also converted back to the anglicized version of his name.

According to *The New Handbook of Texas,* the region surrounding Presidio is the "oldest continuously cultivated area in the United States. Farmers have lived at Presidio since 1500 B.C." It is also one of the hottest spots in the United States, with the thermometer often rising to 117 degrees and higher.

Not one to up and move without purpose, Milton purchased land in 1858 at the locations of three springs: Cibolo ("buffalo"), La Cienega ("marshy place"), and La Morita ("the little mulberry tree"). These locales were the start of a vast cattle and sheep empire that would make Milton a West Texas baron. The waterways he coveted were owned by Juana Pedrasa Leaton y Hall, widow of trader Benjamin Leaton, and A. C. Hyde. Milton bought all rights from the widow for $2,000. From Hyde he secured a warranty deed for $500. The pioneer obtained his first herd of cattle—some three hundred longhorns—from San Pablo, Mexico. Because he never parted with money unless necessary, Milton traded produce from his vast agricultural acreage for any nondomestic needs.

Well aware of the regional Indian problem, and carrying scars from earlier battles south of the border, Milton took steps to protect himself, his family, and his property. Establishing Cibolo Springs as headquarters, he proceeded to build what *The New Handbook* describes as a "100-square-foot adobe block compound with circular defense towers at the north and south corners."

The springs where Milton settled provided water for his stock, and he built *acequias* (irrigation canals) to transport water to his farms and extensive peach orchards. He set up cattle ranches at Cibolo and La Cienega Springs and a sheep ranch at La Morita. He also fortified his enterprise at La Cienega, but not as elaborately as at Cibolo. At the former the stockade was enclosed with eighty-nine-foot walls and lookout towers on the southwest and northeast corners. La Morita was left unprotected, and the inhabitants paid dearly for the oversight: Apaches attacked the ranch and killed many residents. At Cibolo all the rooms were connected, and each had a door that opened onto a vast courtyard. Apparently, Milton hired soldiers to serve as guards at Cibolo, a practice not uncommon at the time.

Milton began his rise in the cattle kingdom by supplying beef to the military at Fort Davis, some eighty miles north of Presidio. The fort was opened in late 1854 to protect travelers along the route from San Antonio to El Paso, an area still thickly populated by Indians at the time.

Once the Civil War started in April 1861, Fort Davis was abandoned. Not only did this eliminate the market for Faver cattle, but with the soldiers gone Indians began attacking area ranches and homesteads with impunity. The fort reopened in 1867 (it was closed for good in 1891), and ranchers started rebuilding their herds. As for Milton, his stock had been reduced to about thirty-two calves. Such setbacks could not deter a man of his perseverance, however. With soldiers back at the fort and the Indian threat steadily diminishing, Milton set out to complete his cattle empire. He registered an F brand for his cattle and eventually expanded his herd to over ten thousand head.

(It has been suggested that Gil Favor, the *Rawhide* character played by Eric Fleming, was based on Milton Faver. Other than the closeness of the last names, this is a stretch. There is no record that Milton was involved in cattle drives, which was the dominant theme of the television production.)

Aggressive and ambitious, Milton was not overly generous with the wages he paid his employees. He hired Mexican labor and paid them a grand wage of 12.5 cents a day to operate his ranches and farms. Even in those days, this was an extremely poor income. On his farms Milton grew practically everything needed to make the Faver domain independent from the outside world. Products he did have to procure he bartered for, penny-pinching when it came to doling out cash.

Milton had fewer than three thousand acres in his name, but he didn't concern himself about pasturing his cattle and sheep. Like many other West Texas ranchers of the day, he let his herd, mostly unbranded, roam the valleys and canyons. Besides, Milton was virtually the undisputed ruler of his empire, the law of the land. He made the rules, saw that they were enforced, and meted out punishment as he saw fit.

While miserly toward his ranch hands and other employees, he was the opposite when it came to his own pockets. He neither believed in nor would accept paper currency. Whenever Milton was due monetary payment, he expected such in gold or silver coin. He was so demanding that as the cattle he was selling were herded through the chute, Milton insisted that the buyer pay for each head as it was counted.

Milton was usually successful in his dealings, be they for livestock or other products. Some, if not much, of his success may have been due to the bottles of peach brandy that were his pride and joy. Milton owned a large peach orchard. He brought a fifty-gallon still made of copper from Chihuahua and perfected a home-brewed brandy over a period of time. Others in the region also produced the fermented peach, but Milton's version, with the aid of his special still, seemed to rise to the top. Whenever he was negotiating for land or livestock, he would take the seller or buyer into his living room; they would light cigars, sit back, and relax. Soon, his Mexican servants would begin pouring brandy for the guests. Plying them with good conversation and drink, Milton had a leg up when they settled down to negotiating.

Milton concentrated his wealth in land and livestock, and he seldom ventured far from his domain. When silver was discovered some five miles south of El Cibolo in the 1880s, Milton held very little land in the area. The site of the strike soon became the town of Shafter, named for Lieutenant Colonel William Shafter, an officer at Fort Davis. Milton did have title to a bit of land at the town limits, but he did not get involved in the silver boom.

John W. Spencer, like Milton originally a freighter, got tired of the bumpy roads, hard wagon seats, and perils presented by Indians. He turned to prospecting. In September 1880 Spencer discovered silver ore in the area. The site never acquired Spencer's name because he took the ore to Shafter, who had it assayed. When the assay proved valuable, Shafter, along with two fellow officers—Lieutenant John L. Bullis (for whom Camp Bullis in San Antonio was named) and Lieutenant Louis Wilhelmi—began purchasing land in the region. The three men agreed to bring John Spencer into the group as an equal partner, although he owned no land.

Their operation was taken over by a California mining group in 1883 and named the Presidio Mining Company. The conglomerate paid three of the partners $1,600 each and five thousand shares of stock for their part in the deal. Bullis refused to sell his land; nevertheless, in 1884 the court approved operation on the Bullis site. The mine opened and closed several times over the ensuing years and was acquired by the American Metal Company in 1928. The mine closed permanently in 1942. Like the mine, the hamlet of Shafter also closed.

Milton had no need to speculate on mineral futures. His livestock count reached a high of around twenty thousand head, some carrying his F brand but probably just as many being mavericks, a practice common in West Texas at the time. Milton's other livestock holdings consisted of horses, oxen, and sheep. Not considering his pasturing land, he counted more than 1,200 acres as usable acreage.

By 1886 Milton was about sixty-four years of age. Time and toil had taken their toll, and he was believed to have suffered from tuberculosis contracted at a younger age. The "King of the West" decided to cut back on his activities and let someone else do the work. He authorized D. G. Knight to take over operation of the ranches and farms for three years. According to *The New Handbook of Texas*, these were the terms of the contract: "Faver would pay the operating expenses for the first year. For his work, Knight would receive every third calf branded and every eighth steer on the range." Due to a fall in the cattle market and low grazing output, Knight realized little return for his three-year effort. The contract was not renewed in 1889, and Milton sold what cattle holdings he had left to Joe Humphreys.

Milton was a livestock man. That is what he wanted to be, and what he became. His mode of transportation was horse or horse-drawn carriage—always. In the 1880s railroad tracks arrived in his region of the country. Milton had an appointment in San Antonio, more than four hundred miles distant. He refused to ride the train for the long, arduous journey. Instead, he rode his horse. For Milton, the iron horse would never replace the one made of bone and blood.

Late in 1889, two days before Christmas, Milton passed away due to natural causes. In accordance with his wishes, he was interred at Chinati Peak, overlooking Big Springs Cibolo Creek.

Milton Faver is gone, but his memory lives on, not only in historical recordings but also in what he left behind. His beloved fort was pulled from the ashcan of ruin, refurbished, and today serves as a tourist getaway called Cibolo Creek Ranch. (It offers all the amenities of comfort, from Jacuzzis to down pillows and handmade quilts, but there are no telephones or television sets in the guestrooms, and electrical appliances are hidden. Perhaps the managers want to preserve a few of the realities of Milton's day.) This thirty-thousand-acre escape from strife and stress is situated west of the town of Presidio, near the entrance to Big Bend National Park.

Bibliography

FATHER MICHAEL MULDOON

Brands, H. W. *Lone Star Nation.* New York: Doubleday, 2004.

"Celtic Cleric." www.users.evi.net/-gpmoran/ch2chtm (accessed May 26, 2005).

Davis, Joe Tom. *Legendary Texians.* Vol. III. Austin: Eakin Press, 1986.

Fehrenbach, T. R. *Lone Star: A History of Texas and the Texans.* New York: Collier Books, 1968.

Golson, Josephine Polley. *Bailey's Light: Saga of Brit Bailey and Other Hardy Pioneers.* San Antonio: The Naylor Company, 1950.

Lamer, Ann. "Father Michael Muldoon." *Footprints of Fayette.* www .rootsweb.com/~txfayett/footprints3.htm (accessed May 26, 2005).

"Religion: 1824–1836." www.bchm.org/Austin/panel133.html (accessed August 19, 2005).

Ruff, Ann. "Miguel Muldoon: Forgotten Padre of Texas." *Texas Highways,* September 1986.

Smithwick, Noah. *The Evolution of a State or Recollections of Old Texas Days.* Austin: University of Texas Press, 1983.

Trigg, Linda. "Father Michael Muldoon: The Story of an Early Pioneer Priest." Master's thesis, St. Mary's University, 1940.

Tyler, Ron, Douglas E. Barnett, Roy R. Barkley, Penelope C. Anderson, and Mark F. Odintz, eds. *The New Handbook of Texas.* Vols. 1, 4, 6. Austin: Texas State Historical Association, 1996.

Vanderholt, Father James. "Padre Miguel Muldoon: The Forgotten Man of Texas History." *Catholic Heritage,* November-December 1993.

SARAH BOWMAN

Elliott, J. F. "The Great Western: Sarah Bowman, Mother and Mistress to the U. S. Army." *Journal of Arizona History* 30, no. 1 (Spring 1989).

Ford, John Salmon. *Rip Ford's Texas.* Austin: University of Texas Press, 1963.

Graf, Mercedes. "Standing Tall with Sarah Bowman: The Amazon of the Border." *Minerva: Quarterly Report on Women and the Military,* Fall-Winter 2001. http://findarticles.com/p/articles/mi_m0EXI/is_2001_Fall-Winter/ai_92588782 (accessed May 28, 2005).

Myers, Cindi. "Speaking of Texas—Sarah, Tough and Tall." *Texas Highways,* February 2002.

Phillips, Lisa, and Reyna Martinez. "Sarah Bowman and Tillie Howard: Madams of the 1800s." *Borderlands: An El Paso Community College Local History Project.* http://www.epcc.edu/nwlibrary/borderlands/18_sarah_bowman.htm (accessed May 28, 2005).

Tyler, Ron, Douglas E. Barnett, Roy R. Barkley, Penelope C. Anderson, and Mark F. Odintz, eds. *The New Handbook of Texas.* Vols. 1, 2. Austin: Texas State Historical Association, 1996.

Wallace, Edward S. "The Great Western." *The Westerners—New York Posse Brand Book.* Vol. 5, No. 3, 1958.

AYLETT C. BUCKNER

Barns, Florence Elberta. "Building a Texas Folk-Epic." *Texas Monthly,* October 1929.

Brands, H. W. *Lone Star Nation.* New York: Doubleday, 2004.

Davis, Joe Tom. *Legendary Texians.* Vol. II. Austin: Eakin Press, 1985.

Hatley, Allen G. "He Should Not Be Forgotten!" *Footprints of Fayette.* www.rootsweb.com/~txfayett/footprints1.htm (accessed October 25, 2005).

Robinson, Charles M. III. *The Men Who Wear the Star: The Story of the Texas Rangers.* New York: Random House, 2000.

Ruckert, Annette. "Aylett C. 'Strap' Buckner." *Footprints of Fayette.* www.rootsweb.com/~txfayett/footprints1.htm (accessed October 25, 2005).

Tyler, Ron, Douglas E. Barnett, Roy R. Barkley, Penelope C. Anderson, and Mark F. Odintz, eds. *The New Handbook of Texas.* Vols. 1-6. Austin: Texas State Historical Association, 1996.

SOPHIA PORTER

Alter, Judy. Review of *Red River Women,* by Sherrie S. McLeRoy. *Southwestern Historical Quarterly* 100, no. 4 (April 1997), 519. www.tsha.utexas.edu/shqonline/apager.php?vol=100&pag=543 (accessed November 11, 2007).

"Lake Texoma Map and Information." www.cantweight.net/texoma info.html (accessed June 26, 2005).

McGuire, Jack. "Sophia Porter: Texas' Own Scarlett O'Hara." In *Legendary Ladies of Texas,* edited by Francis Edward Abernethy, 73-78. Denton: University of North Texas Press, 1994.

McLeRoy, Sherrie. "The Adventures of Sophia." *Texas Highways,* February 1990.

———. *Red River Women.* Plano, TX: Republic of Texas Press, 1996.

Middlebrooks, Audy J., and Glenna Middlebrooks. "Holland Coffee of Red River." *Southwestern Historical Quarterly* 69, no. 2. (October 1965), 145-162. www.tsha.utexas.edu/shqonline/apager.php?vol=069&pag=159 (accessed November 11, 2007).

Middlebrooks, Glenna Parker. "Sophia Coffee: History's Firefly." *True West,* October 1973.

Tyler, Ron, Douglas E. Barnett, Roy R. Barkley, Penelope C. Anderson, and Mark F. Odintz, eds. *The New Handbook of Texas.* Vols. 1, 2, 3, 5. Austin: Texas State Historical Association, 1996.

MOLLIE BAILEY

Barkley, Roy R., and Mark F. Odintz, eds. *The Portable Handbook of Texas.* Austin: Texas State Historical Association, 2000.

Boulware, Narcissa Martin. "Following the Mollie Bailey Circus, Upclose and Personal." I've Been Thinking (column), *Montgomery County (TX) News,* March 12, 2003. www.montgomerycountynews.net/archive01/ivebeenthink03-12-03.htm (accessed May 28, 2005).

Gurasich, Marjorie Akers. *Red Wagons and White Canvas: A Story of the Mollie Bailey Circus.* Austin: Eakin Press, 1988.

Handbook of Texas Online, s.v. "Bailey, Mollie Arline Kirkland." www.tsha.utexas.edu/handbook/online/articles/BB/fba12.html (accessed May 28, 2005).

Hartzog, Martha. "Mollie Bailey: Circus Entrepreneur." In *Legendary Ladies of Texas,* edited by Francis Edward Abernethy, 107-14. Denton: University of North Texas Press, 1994.

Knickerbocker, Barbara Barton. "Good Golly, Aunt Mollie." *Texas Highways,* April 2003.

"Mollie Arline Kirkland Bailey." *Alabama Music Hall of Fame.* www .alamhof.org/baileym.htm (accessed May 28, 2005).

"Mollie Bailey." *Bob Heinonen's Texas Heroes.* www.texasheroes.net/ bailey.html (accessed June 4, 2006).

Schwarz, Frederic D. "1881—President Garfield Shot." *American Heritage* 57, no. 3 (June/July 2006). www.americanheritage. com/articles/magazine/ah/2006/3/2006_3_72.shtml (accessed November 11, 2007).

Troesser, John. "Mollie Bailey, Born Mollie Arline Kirkland: Circus Queen of the Southwest." *Texas Escapes.* http://texasescapes.com/ They-Shoe-Horses-Dont-They/Mollie-Bailey.htm (accessed May 28, 2005).

Wikipedia, s.v. "James Anthony Bailey." http://en.wikipedia.org/wiki/ James_Anthony_Bailey (accessed July 3, 2005).

BASS OUTLAW

Cunningham, Eugene. "Bass Outlaw." *Frontier Times*, vol. 5 (January 1928).

———. "Bass Outlaw—The Little Wolf." *Old West,* Fall 1965.

Hunter, J. Marvin. *The Story of Lottie Deno: Her Life and Times.* Bandera, TX: The 4 Hunters, 1959.

Maguire, Jack. "Texas Rangers: They Keep On a'Coming." *Texas Highways,* October 1985.

Majors, Frederick. "Bass Outlaw Was a Texas Riddle." *The West,* October 1965.

Metz Antique Firearms. "Bass Outlaw's Engraved Colt Frontier Six-Shooter." http://winchesters.biz/photo.php?id=1566_0_2_0_M23 (accessed May 22, 2005).

Metz, Leon Claire. *John Selman: Texas Gunfighter.* New York: Hastings House, 1966.

Paul, Lee. "Bass Outlaw: The Little Wolf." www.theoutlaws.com/outlaws4.htm (accessed May 22, 2005).

Smith, Robert Barr. "Sometime Texas Ranger Bass Outlaw Was Not Really a Bad Man, Just a Bad Man with a Bottle." *Wild West,* August 2005.

Tanner, Karen Holliday, and John D. Tanner Jr. "Lon Oden: The Rhymin' Ranger." *Old West,* Summer 1998. Reprinted in *Texas Ranger Dispatch,* Spring 2002. www.texasranger.org/dispatch/6/LonOden.htm (accessed May 22, 2005).

Utley, Robert M. *Lone Star Justice: The First Century of the Texas Rangers.* New York: Berkley Books, 2002.

LIZZIE JOHNSON WILLIAMS

Crawford, Ann Fears, and Crystal Sasse Ragsdale. *Women in Texas: Their Lives, Their Experiences, Their Accomplishments.* Austin: State House Press, 1992.

Garrett, E. "Pioneer School Teacher Amassed a Fortune." *Frontier Times,* vol. 5, February 1928.

Myers, Cindi. "Speaking of Texas—Taking Stock." *Texas Highways,* December 2001.

Shelton, Emily Jones. "Lizzie E. Johnson: A Cattle Queen of Texas." *Southwestern Historical Quarterly,* January 1947.

Stovall, Frances, Maxine Storm, Louise Simon, Gene Johnson, Dorothy Schwartz, and Dorothy Wimberley Kerbow. *Clear Springs and Limestone Ledges: A History of San Marcos and Hays County.* San Marcos, TX: Hays County Historical Commission, 1986.

Taylor, T. U. "Johnson Institute." *Frontier Magazine*, vol 18, February 1941.

Tyler, Ron, Douglas E. Barnett, Roy R. Barkley, Penelope C. Anderson, and Mark F. Odintz, eds. *The New Handbook of Texas.* Vols. 2, 3, 6. Austin: Texas State Historical Association, 1996.

WILD MAN OF THE NAVIDAD

Anderson, John Q. *Tales of Frontier Texas: 1830-1860.* Dallas: Southern Methodist University Press, 1966.

Awbrey, Betty Dooley, Claude Dooley, and the Texas Historical Commission. *Why Stop? A Guide to Texas Historical Roadside Markers.* Fourth edition. Houston: Lone Star Press, 1999.

Evans, Moses. "Wild Man of the Woods." web.wt.net~morris/evans.htm (accessed May 24, 2005).

Handbook of Texas Online, s.v. "Sublime, TX." www.tsha.utexas.edu/handbook/online/articles/view/SS/hns98.html (accessed May 24, 2005).

McIlvane, Myra Hargrave. "The Wild Man of the Navidad." In *Shadows on the Land: An Anthology of Texas Historical Marker Stories,* 79. Austin: Texas Historical Commission, 1984. www.rootsweb.com/~txrefugi/WildManoftheNavidad.htm (accessed May 24, 2005).

Reese, Randy. "Wild Man of the Navidad: Truth or Tall Tale?" *Victoria (TX) Advocate,* July 23, 2002. www.rootsweb.com/~txrefugi/WildManoftheNavidadVictAdv.htm (accessed May 24, 2005).

Tyler, Ron, Douglas E. Barnett, Roy R. Barkley, Penelope C. Anderson, and Mark F. Odintz, eds. *The New Handbook of Texas.* Vols. 2, 4. Austin: Texas State Historical Association, 1996.

Vine, Katy. "Monster, Inc." *Texas Monthly,* October 2005.

Wolff, Henry Jr. "Wild Man of Navidad—A Local Legend." *Victoria (TX) Advocate,* January 27, 2006.

ADAH ISAACS MENKEN

Abbot, Francis. "The First Tightrope Walker, Jean Francois Blondin." Niagara Falls Museum and The Niagara Parks Commission. www.niagara-info.com/historic.htm (accessed May 6, 2006).

"Adah Isaacs Menken (1835–1868)." *Jewish Virtual Library.* www.jewishvirtuallibrary.org/jsource/biography/AMenken.html (accessed May 29, 2005).

Barca, Dane. "Adah Isaacs Menken: Race and Transgendered Performance in the Nineteenth Century." *MELUS* 29, no. 3-4 (Fall-Winter 2004). http://findarticles.com/p/articles/mi_m2278/is_3-4_29/ai_n9507936 (accessed June 24, 2005).

Barkley, Roy R., and Mark F. Odintz, eds. *The Portable Handbook of Texas.* Austin: Texas State Historical Association, 2000.

Brody, Seymour. "Adah Isaacs Menken: Noted Actress and Poet." In *Jewish Heroes and Heroines of America.* Hollywood, FL: Lifetime Books, 1996. www.fau.edu/library/brody23.htm (accessed May 29, 2005).

Cofran, John. "The Identity of Adah Isaacs Menken: A Theatrical Mystery Solved." *Theatre Survey,* May 31, 1990.

Dickson, Samuel. "Adah Isaacs Menken (1835–1868)." *Virtual Museum of the City of San Francisco.* www.sfmuseum.org/bio/adah.html (accessed May 29, 2005).

Eiselein, Gregory. Review of *Performing Menken: Adah Isaacs Menken and the Birth of Celebrity*, by Renée M. Sentilles. *Legacy: A Journal of American Women Writers* 21, no. 2 (2004): 247-49.

Falk, Bernard. *The Naked Lady, or Storm Over Adah: A Biography of Adah Isaacs Menken*. London: Hutchinson & Company, 1934.

Handbook of Texas Online, s.v. "Menken, Adah Isaacs." www.tsha online.org/handbook/online/articles/MM/fme21.html (accessed May 30, 2005).

"Heenan, John C." *Benicia Living*. www.benicialiving.com/index.php/ weblog/more/john_c_heenan/ (accessed June 6, 2005).

"Heenan, John C." *Hickok Sports*. www.hickoksports.com/biograph/ heenanjohnc.shtml (accessed June 6, 2005).

"John Carmel Heenan." *Heenan Directory*. www.heenan.net/directory/ famous/jcarmel.shtml (accessed June 6, 2005).

Lesser, Allen. *Enchanting Rebel: The Secret of Adah Isaacs Menken*. Port Washington, NY: Kennikot Press, 1947.

Mankowitz, Wolf. *Mazeppa—The Life, Loves and Legends of Adah Isaacs Menken*. New York: Stein and Day, 1982.

"Menken, Adah Isaacs." Women in American History, *Encyclopædia Britannica* search.eb.com/women/articles/Menken_Adah_Isaacs .html (accessed May 29, 2005).

"New Orleans' Other Prodigy." *Sarah's Chess Journal* weblog. http:// batgirl.atspace.com/Adah.html (accessed May 29, 2005).

Palmer, Pamela Lynn. "Adah Isaacs Menken: From Texas to Paris." In *Legendary Ladies of Texas*, edited by Francis Edward Abernethy, 85-94. Denton: University of North Texas Press, 1994.

Rabinowitz, Harold, director. "Women Pioneers." *How Did It Really Happen?* Pleasantville, NY: The Reader's Digest Association, 2000.

"Robert Henry Newell." *Virtual American Biographies*. www.famous americans.net/roberthenrynewell (accessed June 6, 2005).

Tyler, Ron, Douglas E. Barnett, Roy R. Barkley, Penelope C. Anderson, and Mark F. Odintz, eds. *The New Handbook of Texas.* Vol. 4. Austin: Texas State Historical Association, 1996.

Vanmeenen, Karen. "Subjectivity Overload—Documentary Photography Conference." *Afterimage,* March 2001. http://findarticles.com/p/articles/mi_m2479/is_5_28/ai_73640908 (accessed June 5, 2006).

Wallechinsky, David, and Irving Wallace. "Biography of Muse and Poet Adah Isaacs Menken." Parts 1-3. *Trivia-Library.* www.trivia-library.com/b/biography-of-muse-and-poet-adah-isaacs-menken-part-1.htm (accessed June 7, 2005).

THREE-LEGGED WILLIE

Anderson, John Q. *Tales of Frontier Texas: 1830–1860.* Dallas: Southern Methodist University Press, 1966.

Bowman, Bob. "Three-Legged Willie." *Texas Escapes.* http://texasescapes.com/AllThingsHistorical/Three-legged-Willie-BB406.htm (accessed June 11, 2006).

Boyd, Eva Jolene. "Speaking of Texas." *Texas Highways,* February 1988.

Brown, John Henry. *History of Texas from 1685–1892.* Vol. 1. Austin: Jenkins Publishing Company, 1972. Original 1892.

Dabney, Bob. "The Rule of Law vs. Mr. Colt." *Houston Lawyer* 36, no. 4 (January-February 1999). Reprinted in *Texas Ranger Dispatch,* Fall 2002. www.texasranger.org/dispatch/8/RuleLaw.htm (accessed March 19, 2005).

Frantz, Joe B. "An End to the Beginning." *Texas Highways,* May 1986.

Gray, James D. "Robert McAlpin Williamson." *Texas Ranger Dispatch,* Winter 2000. www.texasranger.org/dispatch/2/Willie.htm (accessed June 11, 2006).

Hunter, Marvin J. "Three-Legged Willie Williamson." *Frontier Times* 15, no. 3 (December 1937).

———. publisher. "Three-Legged Willie Williamson." *Frontier Times* 5, no. 10 (July 1928).

Osborne, Rebecca. "Three-Legged Willie: History and Genealogy of Williamson County, Texas." http://three-legged-willie.org (accessed May 23, 2005).

Robinson, Charles M. III. *The Men Who Wear the Star: The Story of the Texas Rangers.* New York: Random House, 2000.

Robinson, Duncan W. *Judge Robert McAlpin Williamson: Texas' Three-Legged Willie.* Austin: Texas State Historical Association, 1948.

Smithwick, Noah. *The Evolution of a State: Or Recollections of Old Texas Days.* Austin: University of Texas Press, 1983.

Syers, Ed, and Larry Hodge. *Backroads of Texas.* 3rd ed. Houston: Gulf Publishing, 1993.

Tyler, Ron, Douglas E. Barnett, Roy R. Barkley, Penelope C. Anderson, and Mark F. Odintz, eds. *The New Handbook of Texas.* Vols. 1, 2, 4, 5, 6. Austin: Texas State Historical Association, 1996.

Utley, Robert M. *Lone Star Justice: The First Century of the Texas Rangers.* New York: Berkley Books, 2002.

Webb, Walter Prescott. *The Texas Rangers: A Century of Frontier Defense.* Austin: University of Texas Press, 1935.

Winningham, George W. "Three Legged Willie." *Frontier Times* 14, no. 2 (November 1936).

MADAM CANDELARIA

Allen, Paula. "Obscure Heroines: Women Overshadowed by Other Alamo Figures." *San Antonio Express News,* November 10, 1996.

Baffle, Kent. "Alamo Magic Woven in Old Woman's Tales." *Dallas Morning News,* October 20, 1985.

Bayne, Charles. "Alamo Survivor." *Macon (GA) Telegraph,* December 13, 1952.

Bond, Mary C. "Article Tells of Woman at Alamo." *Seguin (TX) Gazette,* April 26, 1988.

———. "Letter Continues Story of Woman at Alamo." *Seguin (TX) Gazette,* May 3, 1989.

Bowie, Walter Worthington. *The Bowies and Their Kindred: A Genealogical and Biographical History.* Cottonport, LA: Polyanthos, 1971.

The Daily Light (San Antonio), "Battle of the Alamo: Story Told from Madam Candelaria's Lips," March 8, 1899.

Elfer, Maurice. "Heroine of the Alamo: Madam Candelaria, Unsung Nursed Bowie to the End." *Dallas Morning News,* March 9, 1930.

Fehrenbach, T. R. *Lone Star: A History of Texas and the Texans.* New York: Collier Books, 1968.

Ford, John S. *Origin and Fall of the Alamo, March 6, 1836.* San Antonio: Johnson Brothers Printing Co., 1895.

———. "The Fall of the Alamo." *Dallas Morning News,* n.d.

———. Letter re: Pension for Madam Candelaria, San Antonio, March 25, 1889.

Kubiak, Dan. *Ten Tall Texans: Biographical Essays of Ten Texas Heroes and Founders.* 3rd rev. ed. Austin: The Balcones Co., 1985.

Neva, Leticia. "Madame Candelaria: The Alamo's Unsung Heroine." Speech prepared for Battle of Flowers Speech Tournament, San Antonio, 1986.

Paul, Lee. "Legends of the Alamo." www.theoutlaws.com/unexplained 3.htm (accessed June 11, 2006).

———. "The Alamo: 13 Days of Glory." *Wild West,* February 1996. www.historynet.com/magazines/wild_west/3025721.html (accessed June 11, 2006).

Pearson, Jim B., et al. *Texas: The Land and Its People.* 2nd ed. Dallas: Hendrick-Long, 1978.

Price, Jim. "Last Survivor Died Peacefully." *San Antonio Express News,* March 3, 1986.

Ragsdale, Crystal Sasse. *The Women and Children of the Alamo.* Austin: State House Press, 1994.

Remember the Alamo Monument Association. Proclamation. San Antonio, February 12, 1891.

San Antonio Daily Express, "The Last Voice Hushed: Death of Madam Candelaria Yesterday," February 11, 1899.

Shackford, James Atkins. *David Crockett: The Man and the Legend.* Chapel Hill: University of North Carolina Press, 1956.

State of Texas. Twenty-Second Legislature. *Andrea Castañón de Villaneuva, Known as Madam Candelaria—Act for Relief of.* Austin, 1891.

Stevens, Walter B. *Through Texas: A Series of Interesting Letters.* St. Louis: St. Louis Globe-Democrat, 1892.

Tyler, Ron, Douglas E. Barnett, Roy R. Barkley, Penelope C. Anderson, and Mark F. Odintz, eds. *The New Handbook of Texas.* Vols. 1, 2, 6. Austin: Texas State Historical Association, 1996.

Williams, Amelia. "A Critical Study of the Siege of the Alamo and of the Personnel of Its Defenders." *Southwestern Historical Quarterly* 37, no. 3 (January 1934).

Woolford, Sam. *Woolford's Tales: The Traditional "Last Man."* n.p, n.d.

JAMES BRITON BAILEY

"American History: James Britton Bailey." *Electric Scotland.* www.electricscotland.com/history/america/james_bailey.htm (accessed May 22, 2005).

Auction 6: Lots 1-10. www.dsloan.com/Auctions/A6-/Lots_1_10.html (accessed May 22, 2005).

Awbrey, Betty Dooley, Claude Dooley, and the Texas Historical Commission. *Why Stop? A Guide to Texas Historical Roadside Markers.* Fourth Edition. Houston: Gulf Publishing, 1999.

"Bailey's Prairie Investigation." Paranormal Investigation Report, Case No. 2345-79039. www.webspawner.com/users/baileysprairie invest/ (accessed May 22, 2005).

Davis, Joe Tom. *Legendary Texians.* Vol. II. Austin: Eakin Press, 1985.

Flemmons, Jerry, *Texas Siftings: A Bold and Uncommon Celebration of the Lone Star State.* Fort Worth: Texas Christian University Press, 1995.

Golson, Edward M. "Baileys and Polleys Among Earliest Texas." *Frontier Times* 13, no. 5 (February 1936).

Golson, Josephine Polley. *Bailey's Light: Saga of Brit Bailey and Other Hardy Pioneers.* San Antonio: Naylor Company, 1950.

"Legend of Brit Bailey." *Exploring Texas.* explore.tpwd.state.tx.us/gulf angleton/history.htm (accessed June 11, 2006).

Lewis, Elizabeth W. "Speaking of Texas." *Texas Highways,* June 1992.

Smithwick, Noah. *The Evolution of a State or Recollections of Old Texas.* Austin: University of Texas Press, 1983.

Syers, Ed, and Larry Hodge. *Backroads of Texas.* 3rd ed. Houston: Gulf Publishing, 1993.

Tyler, Ron, Douglas E. Barnett, Roy R. Barkley, Penelope C. Anderson, and Mark F. Odintz, eds. *The New Handbook of Texas.* Vols. 1, 3, 6. Austin: Texas State Historical Association, 1996.

Wikipedia, s.v. "Bailey's Prairie, Texas." http://en.wikipedia.org/wiki/Bailey's_Prairie_Texas (accessed May 22, 2005).

Wolff, Henry Jr. "Brit Bailey Wanted to Be Buried Standing Up." *Victoria (TX) Advocate*, January 29, 2006.

Young, Richard Alan, and Judy Dockrey Young. *Ghost Stories from the American Southwest.* Little Rock: August House Publishers, 1991.

MARTHA WHITE MCWHIRTER

Headden, Susan, and Jeffrey L. Sheler, eds. "Women of the Bible." Special issue, *U. S. News & World Report,* 2005.

James, Eleanor. "Martha White McWhirter (1827–1904)." In *Women in Early Texas,* edited by Evelyn M. Carrington, 180–90. Austin: Jenkins, 1975.

———. "The Santificationists of Belton." *America West,* Summer 1965.

Johnson, Melissa. "The Sanctified Sisters." *Texas Historian,* November 1974.

Meeks, Lindsay. "Texas History 101." *Texas Monthly,* December 2005.

Myers, Cindi. "Speaking of Texas." *Texas Highways,* December 1989.

Kitch, Sally. "The Santificationists." Course description for Women's Roles and the Presence of Gender Equality in Utopian Societies. http://louisville.edu/a-s/english/subcultures/colors/red/g0bedf01/sanctified.html (accessed May 25, 2005).

Smithwick, Noah. *The Evolution of a State or Recollections of Old Texas Days.* Austin: University of Texas Press, 1983.

Tyler, Ron, Douglas E. Barnett, Roy R. Barkley, Penelope C. Anderson, and Mark F. Odintz, eds. *The New Handbook of Texas.* Vols. 1, 6. Austin: Texas State Historical Association, 1996.

Werden, Frieda. "Martha White McWhirter and the Belton Santificationists." In *Legendary Ladies of Texas,* edited by Francis Edward Abernethy, 115-22. Denton: University of North Texas Press, 1994.

Wikipedia, s.v. "John Wesley." http://en.wikipedia.org/wiki/John_Wesley (accessed January 22, 2006).

Wright, Gwendolyn. "The Woman's Commonwealth: Separation, Self, Sharing." *Architectural Association Quarterly,* 1974.

Young, T. R. "Feminist Studies." venus.soci.niu.edu/~archives/SSSI TALK/jan99/0228.html (accessed May 25, 2005).

MILTON FAVER

Boggs, Johnny D. "Pioneer Rancher Milton Faver, the So-Called Mystery Man of the Big Bend, Tamed Harsh West Texas." *Wild West,* February 2006.

Brooks, Tim, and Earle Marsh. *The Complete Directory to Prime Time Network TV Shows, 1946–Present.* New York: Ballantine Books, 1979.

Hunter, J. Marvin, publisher. "Mystery Man of Big Bend Knew Only Own Law." *Frontier Times* 19, no. 2 (November 1931).

Jones, Kathryn. "A Place for Discriminating Dudes." *New York Times,* January 24, 1999.

"Presidio County Historical Markers." *Fort Tours: Presidio County.* www.forttours.com/pages/hmpresidio.asp (accessed April 20, 2006).

Sekules, Kate. "A Rio Grande Refuge." *Food & Wine,* June 1999. www.foodandwine.com/articles/a-rio-grande-refuge (accessed April 20, 2006).

Tyler, Ron, Douglas E. Barnett, Roy R. Barkley, Penelope C. Anderson, and Mark F. Odintz, eds. *The New Handbook of Texas.* Vols. 1, 2, 4, 5. Austin: Texas State Historical Association, 1996.

Index

I

Indians
attacks by, 158
Bailey circus and, 58–59
Karankawa, 31, 141
protection against, 160–61
Tawakoni, 29
Tonkawa, 31
trading with, 38, 39–40, 41
Waco, 29
Williamson's treatment of,
120–21

J

Jimbo (Wild Man of Navidad),
89–91
Johnson, Catharine (Hyde),
77–78
Johnson, Sister, 150
Johnson, Thomas Jefferson,
77–78
Jones, Frank, 65, 68–69, 71–72
Jones Creek, Battle of, 141
Judaism, 98

K

Karankawa Indians, 31, 141
Kerr, Orpheus C., 106
Kirkland, Fannie, 53
Knight, D. G., 164

Knight, Sarah. *See* Bowman,
Sarah

L

Lincoln, George, 20
Long, James, 29

M

Mazeppa performances, 104–6
McMahon, Frank, 74
McWhirter, Martha White,
146–56
death of, 154
family life of, 146–47
financial ventures of,
151–52, 154
generosity of, 153
marriage of, 148–50, 155–56
revelations of, 147–48
Women's Commonwealth
leader, 148–56
memorials, 1, 5, 18
Menken, Adah Isaacs, 94–109
death and funeral, 108
early years of, 96–97
enigma of, 94–96
marriages, 98–103, 106–7
Mazeppa performances,
104–6
poetry of, 99, 108

W

Waco Indians, 29

Webb, Walter Prescott, 86

weddings, 6–7

Wesley, John, 146

Wharton, William H., 11–12, 13

Wild Man of the Woods, 92–93

Wild Man/Woman of Navidad, 87–93

Williams, Hezekiah G., 81–84

Williams, Lizzie Johnson, 76–86

  business affairs, 80–86

  cattle driver, 76–77

  early years of, 77–80

  extravagances, 83

  old age and death of, 84–86

  teaching career, 80, 82

Williamson, Robert M. "Three-Legged Willie"

  criticizing Mexico, 112–16

  death and legacy of, 122–23

  early years of, 110–11

  familial background, 120

  judicial/political career, 117–21

  later life, 121–22

  newspaper career, 111–12

  Ranger career, 116–17

Women's Commonwealth, 148–55

Worth, William, 17–18

Y

Yeti, Texas, 87–93

About The Author

Don Blevins has a master of education degree in Southwestern studies from Texas State University. He is a member of the Texas State Historical Association, the Writers' League of Texas, and the Coalition of Texas Authors. He has also written articles for more than fifty magazines. Don lives in San Marcos, Texas.